Betty Crocker
outdoor
food

100 Recipes for the Way You Really Cook

JG PRESS

Manufactured in China

10 9 8 7 6 5 4 3 2 1

Cover photo: Baby Burgers
(page 38)

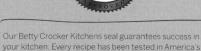

Our Betty Crocker Kitchens seal guarantees success in your kitchen. Every recipe has been tested in America's Most Trusted Kitchens™ to meet our high standards of reliability, easy preparation and great taste.

Dear Friends,

Surf, sand and sun are not the only things that come to mind when we think of summer. The great foods you enjoy at a barbecue, a picnic or an outdoor party help to create the fun and festive mood that accompanies the nice weather. The bounty of fresh fruits, vegetables and herbs that are grown in the summer makes the perfect addition to these great recipes.

You'll find chapters on appetizers and party foods, grilling, picnic-perfect foods, sumptuous side dishes and refreshing drinks. Whether you are feeding your family or the entire block, you will be prepared to please. Brie Quesadillas with Mango Guacamole, Shrimp Deviled Eggs, Chipotle Salsa Ribs, Mediterranean Potato Salad and Frosty Guava-Peach Sippers are just a few of the delicious dishes you can make.

Get ready to enjoy the warm sun and the cool breeze with a feast at your fingertips!

Warmly,

Betty Crocker

contents

Summertime Produce

Treat Yourself to the Season's Best

Summertime is the perfect time to eat plenty of fruits and vegetables. With the amazing palette of colors, plus the crisp and juicy choices available, every eating occasion can be an especially tasty one.

Health experts recommend that we eat five to nine servings of fruits and vegetables each day. Choosing an assortment of these foods gives us a variety of vitamins, minerals and phytonutrients as well as fiber. Together, getting enough of these substances can offer a better chance at better health.

4 Ways to Fit in These All-Stars

- **As a topper:** Slice and diced fruits make terrific toppings for yogurt, cereal, frozen yogurt, angel food cake and pancakes. Roasted or steamed vegetables spruce up baked potatoes, pasta and rice. Top burgers and sandwiches with lettuce and sliced tomatoes or bell peppers.

- **As a mixer:** Toss a handful (or two) of lightly cooked chopped veggies into soups, scrambled eggs, pasta and rice dishes. Add fruit pieces to salads and smoothies.

- **As a side dish:** Forget the chips. Brighten your plate with bite-size berries, sliced cantaloupe or mango or bright green broccoli. Have already-cut produce on hand for afternoon snacks, afterwork munchies or predinner nibbles.

- **As the main event:** Mix favorite fruits or vegetables with light salad dressing, and wrap them up in a whole-grain tortilla or spoon into a pita bread.

Produce That Packs a Punch

Every fruit and vegetable—even iceberg lettuce—has something good to offer, though some pack more nutrition than others. Here are a few of summer's best.

Blueberries: Ranked by the USDA as a top fruit in terms of antioxidant power. Phytonutrient-wise, what's inside may neutralize free radicals and may also help maintain urinary tract health.

Broccoli: Offers calcium, potassium and folate. An excellent source of vitamin C. Contains antioxidants that may neutralize free radicals and disarm some cancer-causing agents.

Cantaloupe: One cup contains 100% of the recommended daily amount of vitamin A (beta-carotene) and vitamin C. Beta-carotene helps keep cells healthy. Some evidence suggests it may help protect the skin from sun damage.

Papaya: Rich in vitamin C and a good source of folate and potassium.

Red bell pepper: An excellent source of vitamin A. Contains more than 100% of the recommended daily amount of vitamin C in ½ cup.

Romaine lettuce: A good source of vitamin C, vitamin A (beta-carotene) and folate. Phytonutrients include zeaxanthin, which may help protect eyes against age-related changes.

Strawberries: 1 cup of whole berries contains 100% of the recommended daily amount of vitamin C. Phytonutrients may help neutralize free radicals and keep cells healthy.

In-Season Herbs

These small garden treasures are packed with distinctive flavors and fragrant aromas that make everyday fare simply extraordinary. Here's a sampler of summer herb favorites.

Basil

Characteristics:

- Intense sweet and spicy flavor, often described as a blend of licorice and cloves.

- Signature herb in Mediterranean and Italian cuisines.

- Available in other varieties, such as lemon, clove, cinnamon and Thai Basil.

Herb Ideas:

- Toss chopped basil with mixed salad greens.

- Sprinkle sliced tomatoes with chopped basil, Parmesan cheese and olive oil.

- Add chopped basil to pasta along with fresh mozzarella and cherry tomatoes.

Chives

Characteristics:

- Bright green with hollow stems.

- Delicate onion flavor.

- Heating chives diminishes their flavor, so add right before serving.

Herb Ideas:

- Sprinkle over grilled or roasted vegetables.

- Stir into cream cheese or cottage cheese.

- Top salads with finely chopped chives.

Cilantro

Characteristics:

- Extremely aromatic with a pungent, acidic flavor.

- Sometimes referred to as Mexican parsley or Chinese parsley.

- This flat-leaf parsley look-alike is a global herb used in Mexican, Indian, Middle Eastern and Asian cuisines.

Herb Ideas:

- Stir into sour cream, salsa or dips.

- Add to chicken salad.

- Top grilled fish with chopped or whole cilantro and lemon or lime juice.

Ginger-Lime Tuna Steaks, page 94

Mint

Characteristics:

- Strong, sweet flavor and cool aftertaste.

- Although "mint" encompasses numerous varieties of this herb, peppermint and spearmint are the most notable.

- Adventurous cooks may want to try chocolate, pineapple and apple mint.

- Peppermint has large, bright green leaves and spearmint has small, dustier gray-green leaves.

Herb Ideas:

- Slightly bruise leaves, and add to your favorite beverage (teas, lemonade, sparkling water).

- Stir chopped mint into chocolate sauce or hot fudge sauce, and serve over cake or ice cream.

- Add chopped mint to fresh peas cooked with butter.

Parsley

Characteristics:

- Distinctive tangy, peppery flavor.

- Most popular in the U.S. is curly leaf parsley, which has small, curly dark green leaves. In most of Europe, however, flat-leaf parsley or Italian parsley, with its flat, dark green leaves, is more popular.

Herb Ideas:

- Stir chopped parsley into tuna salad or egg salad filling for sandwiches.

- Toss with melted butter or olive oil and cooked vegetables.

    - Make a parsley pesto by using half basil and half parsley in your favorite pesto recipe.

Cranberry-Mint Iced Tea,
page 130

Sage Advice

- Homegrown fresh herbs should be picked early in the morning after the dew has evaporated but before the sun is too strong. Pick the tops of the herbs (about 2 to 3 inches) because those leaves contain the most oils.

- Most fresh herbs can be stored in the refrigerator. Wrap stems of fresh herbs in damp paper towel, then put the herbs in a plastic bag and refrigerate.

- For herbs like mint, parsley and cilantro, fill a small jar or glass with about 2 inches of water. Place the stems in the water, and place a plastic bag over the herbs. Secure with a rubber band around the neck of the jar.

- Experimenting with a new herb or adding fresh herbs to a recipe? Use 1 teaspoon of fresh herbs for every four servings the recipe makes. Taste the recipe to decide if you have enough herbs. If you'd like a little more, add a little at a time until the flavor is right.

- Fresh herbs can't be beat, but if you'd like to (or need to) use dried herbs, substitute in a 3-to-1 ratio: for every 3 teaspoons of fresh herbs, you'll need 1 teaspoon of dried herbs.

Herb Blends

The best way to combine different herbs is to experiment, starting with two or three and then adding from there, depending on the recipe. Start with these tried-and-true herb mixtures.

Fines Herbes is terrific for delicately flavored foods like green salads, eggs and cream sauces. Make this with equal parts of summer favorites such as chives, chervil, parsley and tarragon.

Bouquet Garni is a French-inspired herb combination used to flavor soups, stews, casseroles and even rice and grains. Wrap a whole bay leaf, thyme sprig and several parsley sprigs in a small piece of cheesecloth or linen, and tie with string; simmer in the liquid or mixture that you are preparing.

Mixed Herbs are a bit stronger than Fines Herbes so they're used with more robustly flavored foods like meat, fish and some vegetables. Make with equal parts of sage, thyme, marjoram and parsley.

Cheese Tray with Olive Rosemary Skewers

Bread and Spreads Platter

Peachy Cream Cheese–Jalapeño Spread

Five-Layer Mexican Dip

Guacamole-Cheese Crisps

Brie Quesadillas with Mango Guacamole

Taco Mozzi Sticks

Mini Corn Dogs on a Stick

Pesto-Salmon Roulades

Mini Crab Points

Layered Shrimp Spread

Spicy Grilled Shrimp Platter

Planked Salmon Platter

Seafood Salad Tartlets

Basil-Turkey Mini Focaccia Sandwiches

Light Lemon-Dijon Chicken Salad

Cashew Curry Shrimp Salad

Baby Burgers

Mini Barbeque Pizza Wedges

Key Lime Bars

S'mores Chocolate Chip Ice-Cream Sandwiches

Tiramisu Cheesecake Dessert

1

breezy party food

Cheese Tray with Olive Rosemary Skewers

Prep Time: 45 min ▪ Start to Finish: 45 min ▪ 24 Servings

1 round (7 oz) Gouda or Edam cheese
48 to 96 assorted large pitted or stuffed olives (such as kalamata and large
   pimiento-stuffed green olives), drained
24 sprigs rosemary, each 4 inches long
1½ lb assorted cheeses (such as Colby–Monterey Jack, dill Havarti, sharp
   Cheddar and pepper Jack)
Assorted crackers

1 Remove paper and wax from cheese round. On center of 12- to 14-inch platter, place cheese round. Thread 2 to 4 olives on each rosemary sprig. Insert sprigs into cheese round.

2 Cut assorted cheeses into slices and shapes, such as triangles, squares, cubes and sticks; arrange around cheese round. Serve with crackers.

Use thick rosemary sprigs for the skewers so that they won't break. You also can use 3- to 4-inch party picks.

1 Serving: Calories 200 (Calories from Fat 140); Total Fat 15g (Saturated Fat 8g); Cholesterol 40mg; Sodium 400mg; Total Carbohydrate 6g (Dietary Fiber 0g); Protein 9g

Bread and Spreads Platter

Prep Time: 20 min ▮ Start to Finish: 20 min ▮ 18 Servings

    2 containers (8 oz each) chives-and-onion cream cheese spread
    ¼ cup diced drained roasted red bell peppers (from 7-oz jar)
    ¼ cup chopped pimiento-stuffed green olives
    2 tablespoons refrigerated basil pesto (from 7-oz container)
    Leaf lettuce leaves
    1 loaf (20 inch) baguette French bread (12 oz), cut into ¼-inch slices

1 Among 3 small bowls, divide cream cheese. Stir red peppers into cream cheese in 1 bowl. Stir olives into cream cheese in another bowl. Stir pesto into cream cheese in third bowl.

2 Line serving platter with lettuce leaves. Mound 3 spreads on lettuce leaves. Surround with bread slices.

Make little paper flags identifying the three spreads. Then, attach them to toothpicks and place in the spreads.

1 Serving: Calories 140 (Calories from Fat 80); Total Fat 9g (Saturated Fat 5g); Cholesterol 25mg; Sodium 330mg; Total Carbohydrate 11g (Dietary Fiber 0g); Protein 4g

Peachy Cream Cheese–Jalapeño Spread

Prep Time: 15 min ■ Start to Finish: 15 min ■ 8 Servings (2 tablespoons spread and 3 crackers each)

¼ cup peach or apricot preserves
½ red jalapeño chile, seeded, finely chopped
½ green jalapeño chile, seeded, finely chopped
1 package (8 oz) cream cheese, cut in half
Assorted crackers and/or cocktail pumpernickel or rye bread

1 In small bowl, mix preserves and chiles. On small serving plate, place blocks of cream cheese. Spoon preserves mixture over cream cheese.

2 Serve with crackers or cocktail bread.

The remaining chiles can be kept in the refrigerator for several days. Dice a few into taco meat or almost any casserole to add a bit of flavor and heat.

1 Serving: Calories 190 (Calories from Fat 120); Total Fat 13g (Saturated Fat 7g); Cholesterol 30mg; Sodium 190mg; Total Carbohydrate 15g (Dietary Fiber 0g); Protein 3g

Five-Layer Mexican Dip

Prep Time: 20 min ▪ Start to Finish: 20 min ▪ 20 Servings (¼ cup dip and 6 chips each)

1 can (16 oz) refried beans
2 tablespoons chunky-style salsa
1 ½ cups sour cream
1 cup guacamole
1 cup shredded Cheddar cheese (4 oz)
2 medium green onions, chopped (2 tablespoons)
Tortilla chips

1 In medium bowl, mix refried beans and salsa. On 12- or 13-inch serving plate or pizza pan, spread bean mixture in thin layer.

2 Spread sour cream over bean mixture, leaving about 1-inch border of beans around edge. Spread guacamole over sour cream, leaving border of sour cream showing.

3 Sprinkle cheese over guacamole. Sprinkle onions over cheese. Serve immediately, or cover and refrigerate until serving. Serve with tortilla chips.

1 Serving: Calories 150 (Calories from Fat 90); Total Fat 10g (Saturated Fat 4g); Cholesterol 20mg; Sodium 250mg; Total Carbohydrate 13g (Dietary Fiber 2g); Protein 4g

Guacamole-Cheese Crisps

Prep Time: 25 min ■ Start to Finish: 25 min ■ 16 Appetizers

> 1 cup finely shredded Cheddar-Jack with jalapeño peppers cheese blend (from 8-oz package)
> 1 ripe avocado, pitted, peeled and chopped
> 1 tablespoon lime juice
> 1 clove garlic, finely chopped
> 3 tablespoons sour cream
> 3 tablespoons chunky-style salsa

1 Heat oven to 400°F. Line cookie sheet with parchment paper. For each cheese crisp, spoon 2 teaspoons cheese onto paper-lined cookie sheet; pat into 2-inch round. Bake 6 to 8 minutes or until edges are light golden brown. Immediately remove from cookie sheet to wire rack. Cool 5 minutes or until crisp.

2 In small bowl, place avocado, lime juice and garlic; mash avocado with fork and mix with ingredients. Spoon 1½ teaspoons avocado mixture on each cheese crisp; top with about ½ teaspoon each sour cream and salsa.

You can prepare the crisps up to 4 hours ahead of time. Just store them tightly covered at room temperature, then add the topping just before serving.

1 Appetizer: Calories 50 (Calories from Fat 40); Total Fat 4.5g (Saturated Fat 2g); Cholesterol 10mg; Sodium 55mg; Total Carbohydrate 1g (Dietary Fiber 0g); Protein 2g

Brie Quesadillas with Mango Guacamole

Prep Time: 35 min ▮ Start to Finish: 35 min ▮ 24 Servings

Guacamole
1 medium avocado, pitted, peeled and quartered
½ small jalapeño chile, seeded, finely chopped
1 small clove garlic, finely chopped
2 tablespoons lime juice
¼ cup chopped fresh cilantro
⅛ teaspoon salt
½ medium mango, cut in half lengthwise, seed removed, peeled and diced

Quesadillas
6 flour tortillas (8 inch)
1 round (6 to 7 oz) Brie cheese, cut into ⅛-inch strips (not wedges)
¼ lb thinly sliced cooked ham (from deli)
1 tablespoon vegetable oil

1 In food processor, place all guacamole ingredients except mango. Cover; process with 3 or 4 on/off turns until coarsely chopped. Place in small bowl; stir in mango. Set aside.

2 Top half of each tortilla with cheese and ham. Fold tortilla over and press down. Brush top with oil.

3 Heat 12-inch skillet over medium-high heat. Place 3 quesadillas, oil side down, in skillet. Brush tops with half of remaining oil. Cook 2 to 3 minutes, turning once, until both sides are golden brown and cheese is melted. Repeat with remaining quesadillas and oil. Cut each into 4 wedges. Serve with guacamole.

1 Serving: Calories 80 (Calories from Fat 45); Total Fat 5g (Saturated Fat 2g); Cholesterol 10mg; Sodium 190mg; Total Carbohydrate 7g (Dietary Fiber 0g); Protein 3g

If you prefer, you can mash the guacamole ingredients with a fork instead of using a food processor.

Taco Mozzi Sticks

Prep Time: 40 min ▪ Start to Finish: 1 hr 10 min ▪ 8 Servings (2 cheese sticks and
2 teaspoons sauce each)

3 tablespoons milk
3 tablespoons all-purpose flour
1 package (8 oz) mozzarella string cheese (8 sticks), cut crosswise in half
1 egg
3 cups cheese-flavored tortilla chips, crushed (¾ cup crushed)
1 tablespoon taco seasoning mix (from 1.25-oz package)
¾ cup vegetable oil
⅓ cup taco sauce, warmed

1 Line 15×10×1-inch pan with waxed paper. In shallow bowl, place milk. In another shallow bowl, place flour. Dip each stick of string cheese in milk, then coat with flour.

2 Beat egg into remaining milk mixture with fork. In another shallow bowl, mix crushed chips and taco seasoning mix. Dip coated cheese sticks in egg mixture, then coat with chip mixture. Place in pan. Freeze at least 30 minutes but no longer than 8 hours.

3 In 12-inch skillet, heat oil over medium-high heat until 375°F. Cook frozen cheese sticks in oil 1 to 2 minutes on each side, gently turning once or twice, until light golden brown and cheese is warm. Do not overcook or cheese will melt. Serve immediately with warmed taco sauce.

To keep mess to a minimum, place the tortilla chips in a plastic food-storage bag and crush with a rolling pin.

1 Serving: Calories 210 (Calories from Fat 130); Total Fat 14g (Saturated Fat 5g); Cholesterol 40mg; Sodium 380mg; Total Carbohydrate 11g (Dietary Fiber 0g); Protein 9g

Mini Corn Dogs on a Stick

Prep Time: 30 min ▪ Start to Finish: 45 min ▪ 40 Servings (1 corn dog each)

40 wooden toothpicks
1 package (16 oz) cocktail wieners (about 40 pieces)
1 can (12 oz) refrigerated flaky biscuits (10 biscuits)
1 egg, beaten
1 tablespoon milk
½ cup cornmeal
1 tablespoon sugar
¾ cup ketchup
¾ cup yellow mustard

1 Heat oven to 400°F. Grease cookie sheet with shortening or spray with cooking spray. Insert toothpick into narrow end of each wiener. Separate dough into 10 biscuits; carefully divide each biscuit horizontally into 4 rounds. Wrap sides and top of each wiener with dough round, pinching edges to seal.

2 In pie plate, mix egg and milk. On a plate, mix cornmeal and sugar. Roll each wrapped wiener in egg mixture, then roll lightly in cornmeal mixture. Place seam side down on cookie sheet.

3 Bake 10 to 12 minutes or until tops are light golden brown and bottoms are golden brown. Remove from cookie sheet with spatula. Serve with ketchup and mustard.

Don't worry if the dough doesn't wrap perfectly around the hot dogs; it will come together during baking.

1 Serving: Calories 80 (Calories from Fat 40); Total Fat 4.5g (Saturated Fat 1.5g); Cholesterol 10mg; Sodium 310mg; Total Carbohydrate 7g (Dietary Fiber 0g); Protein 2g

Pesto-Salmon Roulades

Prep Time: 15 min ▪ Start to Finish: 15 min ▪ 28 Roulades

1 package (6 oz) smoked salmon lox
⅓ cup refrigerated basil pesto (from 7-oz container)
½ cup drained roasted red bell peppers (from 7-oz jar), cut into thin strips
28 roasted-garlic bagel chips (from 5.5-oz bag)

1 Cut each salmon piece in half lengthwise so that it is about ¾ inch wide. Spread each with about ½ teaspoon of the pesto; top with roasted bell pepper strip. Carefully roll up.

2 Place each roulade on bagel chip. Serve immediately.

Salmon lox is sliced very thinly, so handle the slices carefully to avoid tearing them.

1 Roulade: Calories 30 (Calories from Fat 20); Total Fat 2g (Saturated Fat 0g); Cholesterol 0mg; Sodium 80mg; Total Carbohydrate 1g (Dietary Fiber 0g); Protein 2g

Mini Crab Points

Prep Time: 15 min ■ Start to Finish: 15 min ■ 16 Servings

¼ cup mayonnaise or salad dressing
1 small clove garlic, finely chopped
1 can (6 oz) crabmeat, well drained, flaked
¼ cup finely chopped celery
2 tablespoons diced red bell pepper
2 medium green onions, thinly sliced (2 tablespoons)
¼ teaspoon seafood seasoning (from 6-oz container)
4 slices whole wheat bread, toasted
Chopped fresh parsley

1 In medium bowl, mix mayonnaise and garlic. Stir in crabmeat, celery, bell pepper, onions and seafood seasoning.

2 Top toasted bread with crab mixture. Cut diagonally into quarters. Sprinkle with parsley. Serve immediately.

These garlicky crab appetizers are similar to crab or lobster rolls, sandwiches that are popular across the eastern seaboard.

1 Serving: Calories 50 (Calories from Fat 30); Total Fat 3g (Saturated Fat 0.5g); Cholesterol 10mg; Sodium 100mg; Total Carbohydrate 4g (Dietary Fiber 0g); Protein 3g

Layered Shrimp Spread

Prep Time: 15 min ▪ Start to Finish: 15 min ▪ 16 Servings

1 container (8 oz) pineapple cream cheese spread
½ cup peach or apricot preserves
2 tablespoons cocktail sauce
1 bag (4 oz) frozen cooked salad shrimp, thawed, drained
2 medium green onions, thinly sliced (2 tablespoons)
¼ cup coconut chips
Assorted crackers

1 On 10- to 12-inch serving plate, spread cream cheese to within 1 inch of edge of plate. In small bowl, mix preserves and cocktail sauce. Spread over cream cheese.

2 Top evenly with shrimp. Sprinkle with onions and coconut. Serve with crackers.

Coconut chips are larger than flaked or shredded coconut, so they add more flavor and texture. Look for coconut chips in the baking aisle. You can substitute flaked or shredded coconut, if necessary.

1 Serving: Calories 150 (Calories from Fat 80); Total Fat 8g (Saturated Fat 4g); Cholesterol 25mg; Sodium 240mg; Total Carbohydrate 15g (Dietary Fiber 0g); Protein 4g

Spicy Grilled Shrimp Platter

Prep Time: 20 min ■ Start to Finish: 1 hr 20 min ■ 10 Servings (3 shrimp each)

4 cups water	30 uncooked deveined peeled shrimp
2 tablespoons kosher (coarse) salt	(1¼ lb of 26–30 count size), thawed
2 tablespoons sugar	if frozen, tail shells removed
1 tablespoon crushed red pepper	⅓ cup cocktail sauce
flakes	⅓ cup refrigerated honey mustard dressing
3 cloves garlic, sliced	⅓ cup spicy hot peanut sauce (from 7-oz
1 teaspoon paprika	bottle)

1 In 2-quart saucepan, heat 1 cup of the water to boiling. Add salt, sugar, red pepper flakes, garlic and paprika; stir to dissolve salt.

2 Remove from heat. Add remaining 3 cups cold water. Place shrimp in large resealable food-storage plastic bag. Pour brine mixture over shrimp. Seal bag, pushing out air. Place bag in dish or plastic container. Refrigerate 1 hour.

3 Heat gas or charcoal grill. Remove shrimp from brine mixture; discard brine. On each of 6 (12-inch) metal skewers, thread shrimp, leaving ¼-inch space between each.

4 Place shrimp on grill. Cover grill; cook over medium heat 5 to 6 minutes, turning once, until shrimp are pink.

5 In 3 separate small bowls, place cocktail sauce, dressing and peanut sauce. Arrange bowls on platter; add shrimp to platter.

To broil shrimp, set oven control to broil. Place shrimp on rack in broiler pan. Broil with tops 6 inches from heat 6 to 8 minutes, turning once, until shrimp are pink.

If using bamboo skewers, be sure to soak them in water at least 30 minutes before using so they won't burn during grilling.

1 Serving: Calories 100 (Calories from Fat 45); Total Fat 5g (Saturated Fat 1g); Cholesterol 80mg; Sodium 440mg; Total Carbohydrate 4g (Dietary Fiber 0g); Protein 10g

Planked Salmon Platter

Prep Time: 50 min ■ Start to Finish: 1 hr 50 min ■ 16 Servings

Salmon

1 untreated cedar plank, 12×6 inches

1 salmon fillet, about 1 inch thick (1 lb)

2 tablespoons mayonnaise or salad dressing

2 teaspoons Dijon mustard

1 teaspoon grated lemon peel

Accompaniments

½ cup sour cream

1 teaspoon chopped fresh or ½ teaspoon dried dill weed

1 jar (3.5 oz) small capers, drained

¼ cup spicy brown mustard

2 hard-cooked eggs, finely chopped

1 cup thinly sliced cucumber

32 slices cocktail rye bread

1 Soak cedar plank in water 1 to 2 hours.

2 Heat gas or charcoal grill for indirect-heat cooking as directed by manufacturer. Place salmon, skin side down, on plank. In small bowl, mix mayonnaise, mustard and lemon peel. Brush generously over salmon.

3 Place plank with salmon on grill for indirect cooking. Cover grill; cook over medium heat 25 to 30 minutes or until salmon flakes easily with fork.

4 Remove salmon from plank to platter, using large spatula, or leave salmon on plank and place on large wood cutting board or platter.

5 In small bowl, mix sour cream and dill weed. Place remaining accompaniments except bread in individual small bowls. Place sour cream mixture and remaining accompaniments around salmon. Serve salmon and accompaniments with bread.

To broil salmon, set oven control to broil. Place salmon, skin side down, on rack in broiler pan. (Do not use cedar plank.) Broil with top 6 inches from heat about 15 minutes or until salmon flakes easily with fork.

1 Serving: Calories 120 (Calories from Fat 50); Total Fat 6g (Saturated Fat 2g); Cholesterol 50mg; Sodium 270mg; Total Carbohydrate 8g (Dietary Fiber 0g); Protein 8g

Seafood Salad Tartlets

Prep Time: 15 min ■ Start to Finish: 15 min ■ 30 Tartlets

1 can (6.5 oz) lump crabmeat, drained
1 jar (6.5 oz) marinated artichoke hearts, well drained, finely chopped
    (about 1 cup)
¼ cup chives-and-onion cream cheese spread (from 8-oz container)
2 tablespoons mayonnaise or salad dressing
2 tablespoons chopped red onion
½ teaspoon seafood seasoning
2 packages (2.1 oz each) frozen mini fillo dough shells (30 shells)
30 tiny shrimp (from 4-oz can), rinsed, patted dry
Fresh parsley sprigs

1 In medium bowl, mix crabmeat, artichoke hearts, cream cheese, mayonnaise, onion and seafood seasoning.

2 Just before serving, spoon 1 scant tablespoon crabmeat mixture into each fillo dough shell. Garnish each tartlet with shrimp and parsley.

The frozen fillo dough shells thaw quickly, so there's no need to defrost them ahead.

1 Tartlet: Calories 35 (Calories from Fat 15); Total Fat 1.5g (Saturated Fat 0.5g); Cholesterol 10mg; Sodium 80mg; Total Carbohydrate 3g (Dietary Fiber 0g); Protein 2g

Basil-Turkey Mini Focaccia Sandwiches

Prep Time: 20 min ▮ Start to Finish: 1 hr 5 min ▮ 40 Mini Sandwiches

Focaccia

1 can (13.8 oz) refrigerated pizza crust dough
1 tablespoon olive or vegetable oil
½ teaspoon garlic powder
½ teaspoon Italian seasoning
¼ cup shredded Parmesan cheese (1 oz)

Filling

1 container (6.5 oz) garlic-and-herbs spreadable cheese, softened
2 medium plum (Roma) tomatoes, thinly sliced
1 package (1 oz) fresh basil leaves, stems removed
½ lb thinly sliced smoked turkey breast (from deli)

1 Heat oven to 400°F. Grease large cookie sheet with shortening or cooking spray. Unroll pizza crust dough; press into 12×8-inch rectangle on cookie sheet. With end of handle of wooden spoon, press indentations in top, about 1 inch apart. Brush dough with oil. Sprinkle with garlic powder, Italian seasoning and Parmesan cheese.

2 Bake 10 to 13 minutes or until golden brown. Cool 30 minutes; cut in half horizontally.

3 Spread cut side of bottom of focaccia with spreadable cheese. Top with single layer of tomatoes and basil. Layer turkey evenly over basil. Place top of focaccia, cut side down, over turkey; press down. Pierce through all layers with toothpicks, placing them every 1 ½ inches over focaccia. With long serrated knife, cut between toothpicks into squares.

1 Sandwich: Calories 50 (Calories from Fat 25); Total Fat 2.5g (Saturated Fat 1.5g); Cholesterol 10mg; Sodium 160mg; Total Carbohydrate 5g (Dietary Fiber 0g); Protein 2g

Use purchased focaccia bread, if you prefer. Most store-bought focaccia bread is round, so the number of appetizers will vary.

Light Lemon-Dijon Chicken Salad

Prep Time: 20 min ■ Start to Finish: 20 min ■ 4 Servings

Lemon-Dijon Dressing

¼ cup reduced-fat mayonnaise or salad dressing

2 tablespoons lemon juice

2 teaspoons Dijon mustard

1 clove garlic, finely chopped

Chicken Salad

4 cups shredded romaine lettuce

2 cups shredded cooked chicken breasts

¼ cup sliced drained oil-packed sun-dried tomatoes

1 hard-cooked egg, chopped

2 medium green onions, sliced (2 tablespoons)

¼ cup shredded Parmesan cheese, if desired

1 In small bowl, mix all dressing ingredients with wire whisk.

2 Arrange lettuce, chicken, tomatoes and egg on individual serving plates. Spoon dressing over top. Sprinkle with onions and cheese.

To easily remove the skin from a garlic clove, press the clove firmly with the broad side of a chef's knife, then slice off the ends. The skin will pop right off.

1 Serving: Calories 210 (Calories from Fat 100); Total Fat 11g (Saturated Fat 2g); Cholesterol 115mg; Sodium 260mg; Total Carbohydrate 6g (Dietary Fiber 2g); Protein 24g

Cashew Curry Shrimp Salad

Prep Time: 15 min ∎ Start to Finish: 2 hrs 15 min ∎ 4 Servings

Curry Dressing
½ cup reduced-fat mayonnaise or salad dressing
2 tablespoons lemon juice
1 tablespoon milk
1 teaspoon curry powder
⅛ teaspoon pepper

Shrimp Salad
1 cup frozen sweet peas
1 package (12 oz) frozen cooked deveined peeled shrimp, thawed, drained, tail
   shells removed
2 medium stalks celery, thinly sliced
1 can (1.75 oz) shoestring potatoes
½ cup cashew halves
1 head Belgian endive

1 In small bowl, mix all dressing ingredients with wire whisk.

2 Cook and drain peas as directed on bag. In medium bowl, place peas, shrimp and celery. Add dressing; toss to coat. Cover; refrigerate at least 2 hours to blend flavors.

3 Just before serving, gently stir shoestring potatoes and cashews into shrimp mixture. Arrange endive leaves around edge of medium serving platter. Spoon shrimp mixture into center of platter.

1 Serving: Calories 390 (Calories from Fat 210); Total Fat 23g (Saturated Fat 4.5g); Cholesterol 175mg; Sodium 470mg; Total Carbohydrate 21g (Dietary Fiber 4g); Protein 24g

Baby Burgers

Prep Time: 30 min ∎ Start to Finish: 30 min ∎ 16 Appetizer Burgers

1 lb lean (at least 80%) ground beef
2 teaspoons dried minced onion
1 teaspoon parsley flakes
¾ teaspoon seasoned salt
4 slices (1 oz each) American cheese,
    cut into quarters
8 slices white bread, toasted, crusts
    removed, cut into quarters

16 thin slices plum (Roma) tomatoes
    (2 small), if desired
16 thin hamburger-style dill pickle
    slices, if desired
Ketchup, if desired
Mustard, if desired

1 Heat gas or charcoal grill. In medium bowl, mix beef, onion, parsley flakes and seasoned salt. Divide into 16 portions. Shape each portion into a ball and flatten to ½-inch-thick patty, about 1 ½ inches in diameter. On each of 4 (12-inch) metal skewers, thread 4 patties horizontally, leaving space between each.

2 Place patties on grill. Cover grill; cook over medium heat 8 to 10 minutes, turning once, until patties are no longer pink in center (160°F).

3 Top each burger with cheese piece. Place each burger on toast square. Top with tomato slice and another toast square. Place pickle slice on top; spear with toothpick to hold layers together. Serve with ketchup and mustard for dipping.

To broil patties, set oven control to broil. Thread patties on skewers as directed. Place patties on rack in broiler pan. Broil with tops 6 inches from heat 8 to 10 minutes, turning once, until no longer pink in center.

These cute little burgers can be mixed and shaped ahead of time. Just cover and refrigerate them until you are ready to grill.

1 Burger: Calories 110 (Calories from Fat 50); Total Fat 6g (Saturated Fat 2.5g); Cholesterol 25mg; Sodium 270mg; Total Carbohydrate 7g (Dietary Fiber 0g); Protein 8g

Mini Barbecue Pizza Wedges

Prep Time: 10 min ■ Start to Finish: 20 min ■ 12 Wedges (2 pizzas)

1 package (10 oz) prebaked Italian pizza crusts (6 inch)
¼ cup barbecue sauce
½ cup chopped cooked chicken
1 tablespoon chopped red onion
1 cup finely shredded mozzarella cheese (4 oz)
6 cherry tomatoes, thinly sliced (⅛ cup)

1 Heat gas or charcoal grill for indirect-heat cooking as directed by manufacturer. Top pizza crusts with remaining ingredients in order given.

2 Place pizzas on grill for indirect cooking. Cover grill; cook over medium heat 8 to 10 minutes, rotating pizzas occasionally, until cheese is melted and pizzas are hot. Cut each into 6 wedges.

1 Wedge: Calories 110 (Calories from Fat 35); Total Fat 4g (Saturated Fat 2g); Cholesterol 15mg; Sodium 230mg; Total Carbohydrate 13g (Dietary Fiber 0g); Protein 7g

Key Lime Bars

Prep Time: 15 min ∎ Start to Finish: 4 hrs 20 min ∎ 36 Bars

1½ cups graham cracker crumbs (24 squares)
⅓ cup butter or margarine, melted
3 tablespoons sugar
1 package (8 oz) cream cheese, softened
1 can (14 oz) sweetened condensed milk
1 tablespoon grated lime peel
¼ cup Key lime juice or regular lime juice
Additional lime peel, if desired

1 Heat oven to 350°F. Grease bottom and sides of 9-inch square pan with shortening or cooking spray.

2 In small bowl, mix cracker crumbs, butter and sugar thoroughly with fork. Press evenly in bottom of pan. Refrigerate while preparing cream cheese mixture.

3 In small bowl, beat cream cheese with electric mixer on medium speed until light and fluffy. Gradually beat in milk until smooth. Beat in lime peel and lime juice. Spread over layer in pan.

4 Bake about 35 minutes or until center is set. Cool 30 minutes. Cover loosely; refrigerate at least 3 hours until chilled. For bars, cut into 6 rows by 6 rows. Garnish with additional lime peel. Store covered in refrigerator.

1 Bar: Calories 90 (Calories from Fat 45); Total Fat 5g (Saturated Fat 3g); Cholesterol 15mg; Sodium 65mg; Total Carbohydrate 10g (Dietary Fiber 0g); Protein 2g

S'Mores Chocolate Chip Ice-Cream Sandwiches

Prep Time: 15 min ∎ Start to Finish: 3 hr 15 min ∎ 8 Sandwiches

About 3 tablespoons marshmallow creme
16 fudge-covered graham cookies (1½ × 1 ¾ inches each)
½ cup chocolate chip ice cream

1 Spoon about 1 teaspoon marshmallow creme on 1 cookie. Top with about ½ tablespoon ice cream. Top with another cookie, pressing gently. Place in shallow pan; immediately place in freezer. Repeat for remaining sandwiches, placing each in freezer as made.

2 Freeze at least 3 hours until firm. Wrap individually in plastic wrap or waxed paper.

These frozen treats make a fun summer dessert. To serve a crowd, make a double or triple batch.

1 Sandwich: Calories 100 (Calories from Fat 40); Total Fat 4.5g (Saturated Fat 3.5g); Cholesterol 0mg; Sodium 50mg; Total Carbohydrate 13g (Dietary Fiber 0g); Protein 0g

Tiramisu Cheesecake Dessert

Prep Time: 20 min ■ Start to Finish: 2 hrs 25 min ■ 24 Servings

2 cups crushed vanilla wafer cookies (about 40 cookies)
⅛ cup butter or margarine, melted
2 tablespoons whipping cream
2 tablespoons instant espresso coffee granules
3 packages (8 oz each) cream cheese, softened
¾ cup sugar
3 eggs
1 oz bittersweet baking chocolate, grated
Chocolate-covered espresso beans, if desired

1 Heat oven to 350°F. Line 13×9-inch pan with foil; spray with cooking spray. In small bowl, mix crushed cookies and melted butter with fork. Press mixture in bottom of pan. Refrigerate while continuing with recipe.

2 In small bowl, mix whipping cream and coffee granules with fork until coffee is dissolved; set aside.

3 In large bowl, beat cream cheese with electric mixer on medium speed 2 to 3 minutes, scraping bowl occasionally, until smooth and creamy. On low speed, beat in sugar, eggs and coffee mixture, about 30 seconds. Beat on medium speed about 2 minutes longer or until ingredients are well blended. Using rubber spatula, spread cream cheese filling over crust. Bake 25 to 35 minutes or until center is set.

4 Cool 30 minutes. Sprinkle with grated chocolate or top with espresso beans. Refrigerate about 1 hour or until completely chilled. For servings, cut into 6 rows by 4 rows, using sharp knife dipped in water.

1 Serving: Calories 200 (Calories from Fat 140); Total Fat 15g (Saturated Fat 9g); Cholesterol 65mg; Sodium 140mg; Total Carbohydrate 12g (Dietary Fiber 0g); Protein 4g

In a hurry?
Sift unsweetened baking cocoa over the tiramisu bars instead of grating chocolate.

Sweet and Salty Snack Mix

Ranch Pretzel Nibblers

Chilly Garden Pizza

Caesar Vegetable Dip

Shrimp Deviled Eggs

Tiny Meat and Cheese Bites

Chicken Salad Roll-Ups

Dilly Ham and Cheese Sandwiches

Caesar Focaccia Subs

Curried Egg Salad Sandwiches

Italian Country Sandwich

Italian Chicken Salad

Deli Beef and Bean Tossed Salad

Beef Fajita Pitas

Fresh Fruit Medley

Angel Berry Summer Pudding

Malted Milk Ball Cupcakes

Nutty Chocolate Chip Picnic Cake

Make sure leftovers are refrigerated in a cold cooler within 2 hours
of cooking or removal from the refrigerator. If not, throw them out.

2
picnic portables

Sweet and Salty Snack Mix

Prep Time: 10 min   Start to Finish: 10 min   20 Servings (¼ cup each)

1 package (8 oz) yogurt-covered raisins (1 cup)
2 cups roasted salted soy nuts
1 cup candy-coated peanut butter and chocolate candies
1 cup teddy bear-shaped chocolate graham snacks

1 Mix all ingredients in large bowl or resealable plastic food-storage bag.

You can make this crunchy snack up to one month ahead of time. Store it in small resealable plastic food-storage bags or in an airtight container.

1 Serving: Calories 160 (Calories from Fat 60); Total Fat 7g (Saturated Fat 3g); Cholesterol 0mg; Sodium 50mg; Total Carbohydrate 19g (Dietary Fiber 2g); Protein 5g

Ranch Pretzel Nibblers

Prep Time: 5 min   Start to Finish: 45 min   16 Servings (½ cup each)

1 package (14 oz) sourdough pretzel nuggets (about 5 cups)
3 cups checkerboard pretzels or mini-pretzel twists
⅓ cup vegetable oil
1 package (1 oz) ranch dressing mix

1 Heat oven to 325°F. In ungreased 15×10×1-inch pan, place pretzels. In small bowl, mix oil and dressing mix. Pour over pretzels; stir to coat.

2 Bake 10 minutes, stirring once. Cool completely, about 30 minutes. Store tightly covered.

1 Serving: Calories 170 (Calories from Fat 50); Total Fat 6g (Saturated Fat 1g); Cholesterol 0mg; Sodium 680mg; Total Carbohydrate 27g (Dietary Fiber 1g); Protein 3g

Chilly Garden Pizza

Prep Time: 15 min   Start to Finish: 15 min   6 Servings

1 container (6.5 oz) 50%-less-fat garlic-and-herbs spreadable cheese
1 package (10 oz) prebaked thin Italian pizza crust (12 inch)
¾ cup chopped fresh spinach
½ cup diced seeded cucumber
1 large tomato, chopped (1 cup)
½ cup sliced fresh mushrooms
1 tablespoon chopped fresh basil leaves
¼ teaspoon salt
⅛ teaspoon pepper
¾ cup shredded carrot

1 Spread cheese over pizza crust.

2 Top with spinach, cucumber, tomato, mushrooms and basil. Sprinkle with salt and pepper. Top with carrot.

Enjoy the bounty of your garden and get your vitamins and minerals, too. Spinach is loaded with vitamin A, and tomatoes are a vitamin C powerhouse.

1 Serving: Calories 220 (Calories from Fat 80); Total Fat 8g (Saturated Fat 4g); Cholesterol 15mg; Sodium 420mg; Total Carbohydrate 29g (Dietary Fiber 2g); Protein 7g

Caesar Vegetable Dip

Prep Time: 5 min   Start to Finish: 35 min   10 Servings

½ cup sour cream
¼ cup mayonnaise or salad dressing
¼ cup creamy Caesar dressing
¼ cup shredded Parmesan cheese
1 leaf romaine lettuce
3 tablespoons slightly crushed croutons (about 6)
Assorted raw vegetables

1 In small bowl, mix sour cream, mayonnaise and Caesar dressing until smooth. Stir in cheese. Cover and refrigerate 30 minutes to blend flavors.

2 Line serving bowl with lettuce leaf. Spoon dip into bowl. Sprinkle with crushed croutons. Serve with vegetables.

Keep this dip chilled while serving, place the serving bowl on a bed of ice.

1 Serving: Calories 70 (Calories from Fat 40); Total Fat 4.5g (Saturated Fat 2g); Cholesterol 10mg; Sodium 180mg; Total Carbohydrate 5g (Dietary Fiber 2g); Protein 3g

Shrimp Deviled Eggs

Prep Time: 40 min   Start to Finish: 50 min   12 Appetizers

6 eggs
2 medium green onions, thinly sliced (2 tablespoons)
¼ cup reduced-fat mayonnaise or salad dressing
1 tablespoon white vinegar
¼ teaspoon salt
¼ teaspoon red pepper sauce
½ cup coarsely chopped cooked salad shrimp, thawed if frozen
1 tablespoon cocktail sauce

1 Place eggs in single layer in 2-quart saucepan; add enough cold water so it is at least 1 inch above eggs. Heat to boiling; remove from heat. Cover and let stand 18 minutes. Drain; rinse with cold water. Let stand in ice water 10 minutes.

2 Peel eggs; cut in half lengthwise. Slip out yolks; place in medium bowl. Mash yolks with fork until smooth. Reserve 1 teaspoon green part of onions for garnish. Stir mayonnaise, vinegar, salt, pepper sauce and remaining green onions into mashed yolks. Fold in shrimp.

3 Fill egg whites with yolk mixture, heaping it lightly. Just before serving, top with cocktail sauce and reserved green onions.

To keep your eggs from tipping over when you serve them, cut a very thin slice from the rounded bottom of each egg half. This will make the eggs more stable. If transporting these deviled eggs, prepare ahead and refrigerate 2 hours or until thoroughly chilled. Then, place in an insulated cooler with plenty of ice packs.

1 Appetizer: Calories 80 (Calories from Fat 60); Total Fat 6g (Saturated Fat 1.5g); Cholesterol 130mg; Sodium 150mg; Total Carbohydrate 1g (Dietary Fiber 0g); Protein 5g

Tiny Meat and Cheese Bites

Prep Time: 40 min   Start to Finish: 40 min   40 Appetizers

1 cup pickled vegetable mix (from 16-oz jar), drained
40 cubes (½ inch) hard salami (about ½ lb)
40 cubes (½ inch) Swiss cheese (about ¼ lb)

1 Cut larger pieces of vegetable mix into ½-inch pieces.

2 Alternate pieces of salami, vegetables and cheese on toothpicks.

1 Appetizer: Calories 35 (Calories from Fat 25); Total Fat 2.5g (Saturated Fat 1g); Cholesterol 5mg; Sodium 115mg; Total Carbohydrate 0g (Dietary Fiber 0g); Protein 2g

Chicken Salad Roll-Ups

Prep Time: 35 min   Start to Finish: 1 hr 35 min   24 Appetizers

2 cups chopped cooked chicken
3 medium green onions, chopped (3 tablespoons)
¼ cup chopped walnuts
½ cup creamy poppy seed dressing
½ cup cream cheese spread (from 8-oz container)
2 flour tortillas (10 inch)
6 leaves Bibb lettuce
½ cup finely chopped strawberries

1 In food processor bowl, mix chicken, onions and walnuts. Cover and process by using quick on-and-off motions until finely chopped. Add ½ cup of the poppy seed dressing; process only until mixed. In small bowl, mix remaining dressing and the cream cheese with spoon until smooth.

2 Spread cream cheese mixture evenly over entire surface of tortillas. Remove white rib from lettuce leaves. Press lettuce into cream cheese, tearing to fit and leaving top 2 inches of tortillas uncovered. Spread chicken mixture over lettuce. Sprinkle strawberries over chicken.

3 Firmly roll up tortillas, beginning at bottom. Wrap each roll in plastic wrap. Refrigerate at least 1 hour. Trim ends of each roll. Cut rolls into ½- to ¾-inch slices.

If transporting this appetizer, place the slices in a covered container in an insulated cooler with plenty of ice packs to keep them cold until ready to serve.

1 Appetizer: Calories 70 (Calories from Fat 35); Total Fat 4g (Saturated Fat 1.5g); Cholesterol 20mg; Sodium 50mg; Total Carbohydrate 5g (Dietary Fiber 0g); Protein 4g

Dilly Ham and Cheese Sandwiches

Prep Time: 45 min ▪ Start to Finish: 45 min ▪ 32 Appetizers

1 cup garlic-and-herbs spreadable cheese (from 6.5-oz container)
32 slices cocktail pumpernickel bread
½ lb shaved or very thinly sliced baked ham (from deli)
1 seedless cucumber, very thinly sliced
Fresh dill weed, if desired

1 Spread about 1½ teaspoons cheese on each bread slice. Top with ham, folded to fit, and 2 cucumber slices.

2 Garnish with tiny sprigs of dill.

Make these sandwiches a day ahead, then store them in a single layer in a totable container. Keep them in your fridge until you're ready to go.

1 Appetizer: Calories 50 (Calories from Fat 25); Total Fat 2.5g (Saturated Fat 1.5g); Cholesterol 10mg; Sodium 150mg; Total Carbohydrate 4g (Dietary Fiber 0g); Protein 3g

Caesar Focaccia Subs

Prep Time: 25 min   Start to Finish: 25 min   24 Servings

3 round Italian focaccia breads (about 10 inches in diameter)
1 cup Caesar dressing
12 to 20 leaves romaine lettuce
12 oz thinly sliced smoked turkey
12 oz thinly sliced salami
12 oz sliced smoked provolone cheese

1 Cut each bread in half horizontally. Drizzle dressing evenly over cut sides of bottom and top halves of bread.

2 Layer lettuce, turkey, salami and cheese on bottom halves. Top with top halves. Secure loaves with toothpicks or small skewers. Cut each loaf into 8 wedges.

For a flavor boost, try preparing subs with specialty focaccia bread, such as sun-dried tomato or spinach-Parmesan.

1 Serving: Calories 310 (Calories from Fat 160); Total Fat 18g (Saturated Fat 5g); Cholesterol 30mg; Sodium 810mg; Total Carbohydrate 24g (Dietary Fiber 1g); Protein 13g

Curried Egg Salad Sandwiches

Prep Time: 15 min   Start to Finish: 15 min   2 Sandwiches

3 hard-cooked eggs, chopped
¼ cup fat-free mayonnaise or salad dressing
¼ teaspoon salt
¼ teaspoon curry powder
¼ cup shredded carrot
2 tablespoons finely chopped onion
2 tablespoons coarsely chopped cashews
4 slices whole-grain bread

1 In small bowl, stir together all ingredients except bread.

2 Spread egg mixture on 2 slices bread. Top with remaining bread.

Prepare these perfectly portable sandwiches in advance. Make the egg salad the night before, and assemble sandwiches in the morning. Add an ice pack to your lunch box or picnic basket, and you're ready to go.

1 Sandwich: Calories 340 (Calories from Fat 140); Total Fat 15g (Saturated Fat 4g); Cholesterol 320mg; Sodium 960mg; Total Carbohydrate 36g (Dietary Fiber 5g); Protein 17g

Italian Country Sandwich

Prep Time: 10 min   Start to Finish: 10 min   4 Servings

1 uncut loaf (1 lb) Italian peasant-style rustic bread or ciabatta bread
⅓ cup rosemary-flavored or plain olive oil
¼ lb hard salami, thinly sliced
¼ lb sliced provolone cheese
¼ lb thinly sliced prosciutto
1 small red onion, thinly sliced

1 Cut bread loaf in half horizontally. Drizzle oil over cut sides of bread.

2 Layer salami, cheese, prosciutto and onion on bottom of bread; add top of bread. Cut loaf into 4 pieces.

Make your own rosemary olive oil: In a small saucepan, warm 1 cup olive oil with 1 or 2 sprigs of washed and dried fresh rosemary for 8 to 10 minutes. Cool; discard rosemary. Pour oil into a jar with a tight-fitting lid. Store in refrigerator up to 2 weeks.

1 Serving: Calories 740 (Calories from Fat 380); Total Fat 42g (Saturated Fat 13g); Cholesterol 60mg; Sodium 1860mg; Total Carbohydrate 60g (Dietary Fiber 3g); Protein 30g

Italian Chicken Salad

Prep Time: 10 min   Start to Finish: 10 min   24 Servings (¾ cup each)

4 cups cut-up cooked chicken
2 bags (10 oz each) ready-to-eat Italian-blend salad greens
2 cans (14 oz each) artichoke hearts, drained, chopped
2 cans (4.25 oz each) chopped ripe olives
½ cup zesty Italian dressing

1 In very large (9-quart) bowl, mix all ingredients except dressing.

2 Toss salad with dressing until coated.

Keep salad cold during transporting by placing the covered bowl in an insulated cooler with plenty of ice packs. Place on serving table just before serving.

1 Serving: Calories 100 (Calories from Fat 45); Total Fat 5g (Saturated Fat 1g); Cholesterol 20mg; Sodium 230mg; Total Carbohydrate 5g (Dietary Fiber 2g); Protein 8g

Deli Beef and Bean Tossed Salad

Prep Time: 10 min   Start to Finish: 10 min   6 Servings

1 bag (10 oz) mixed salad greens
1 can (15 oz) three-bean salad, chilled, or 1 pint (2 cups) three-bean salad
   (from deli)
¼ lb cooked roast beef (from deli), cut into julienne strips (¾ cup)
1 cup shredded Cheddar or Swiss cheese (4 oz)
12 cherry tomatoes, cut in half

1 In large bowl, toss all ingredients.

1 Serving: Calories 170 (Calories from Fat 80); Total Fat 9g (Saturated Fat 5g); Cholesterol 30mg; Sodium 420mg; Total Carbohydrate 12g (Dietary Fiber 3g); Protein 11g

Beef Fajita Pitas

Prep Time: 10 min   Start to Finish: 10 min   4 Servings

¼ cup chunky-style salsa
2 pita breads (6 inch), cut in half to form pockets
¾ lb thinly sliced cooked roast beef (from deli)
1 small red bell pepper, cut into ¼-inch strips
4 slices (1 oz each) Monterey Jack cheese

1 Spoon salsa into pita bread halves.

2 Fill pita breads with beef, bell pepper and cheese.

For a more authentic Mexican flavor, sprinkle the pitas with chopped fresh cilantro.

1 Serving: Calories 340 (Calories from Fat 120); Total Fat 13g (Saturated Fat 7g); Cholesterol 95mg; Sodium 440mg; Total Carbohydrate 19g (Dietary Fiber 1g); Protein 37g

Fresh Fruit Medley

Prep Time: 20 min   Start to Finish: 20 min   12 Servings

Honey-Poppy Seed Dressing
¼ cup vegetable oil
3 tablespoons honey
2 tablespoons lemon juice
1½ teaspoons poppy seed

Fruits
2 nectarines or apricots, sliced
1 orange, peeled, sliced
1 medium pineapple, peeled, cored and cut into 1-inch pieces
1 small bunch seedless grapes, each cut in half (2 cups)

1 In tightly covered container, shake all dressing ingredients. Shake again before pouring over fruits.

2 In large bowl, toss fruits and dressing. Cover and refrigerate until ready to serve.

Use a mixture of red and green grapes to add color to the fruit medley.

1 Serving: Calories 110 (Calories from Fat 45); Total Fat 5g (Saturated Fat 0.5g); Cholesterol 0mg; Sodium 0mg; Total Carbohydrate 16g (Dietary Fiber 1g); Protein 0g

Angel Berry Summer Pudding

Prep Time: 25 min   Start to Finish: 4 hrs 25 min   12 Servings

2 boxes (4-serving size each) vanilla instant pudding and pie filling mix
4 cups milk
¾ teaspoon rum extract
1 round angel food cake (10 inch), torn into bite-size pieces
4 cups sliced fresh strawberries
2 cups fresh raspberries
Frozen (thawed) whipped topping, if desired

1 Make pudding mixes as directed on package for pudding, using 4 cups milk and adding rum extract.

2 In 13×9-inch glass baking dish, spoon ⅓ of the pudding. Layer with half of the cake pieces and half of the berries. Repeat layers, ending with remaining pudding.

3 Cover and refrigerate at least 4 hours. Garnish each serving with a dollop of whipped topping.

This recipe is perfect to tote to a casual picnic. Place the covered container in an insulated cooler with plenty of ice packs to keep it cold until serving time.

1 Serving: Calories 260 (Calories from Fat 20); Total Fat 2g (Saturated Fat 1g); Cholesterol 5mg; Sodium 650mg; Total Carbohydrate 57g (Dietary Fiber 3g); Protein 7g

Malted Milk Ball Cupcakes

Prep Time: 20 min   Start to Finish: 1 hr 25 min   24 Cupcakes

Cupcakes

1 box yellow cake mix
1 cup malted milk balls, coarsely crushed
¼ cup natural-flavor malted milk powder
1¼ cups water
⅓ cup vegetable oil
3 eggs

Frosting and Garnish

¼ cup butter or margarine, softened
2 cups powdered sugar
2 tablespoons natural-flavor malted milk powder
1 tablespoon unsweetened baking cocoa
2 tablespoons milk
1⅔ cups malted milk balls, coarsely crushed

1 Heat oven to 350°F. Place paper baking cup in each of 24 regular-size muffin cups. In large bowl, mix cake mix, 1 cup malted milk balls and ¼ cup malted milk powder. Add water, oil and eggs. Beat with electric mixer on low speed 2 minutes. Divide batter evenly among muffin cups.

2 Bake 18 to 23 minutes or until toothpick inserted in center comes out clean. Cool 10 minutes; remove from pan to wire rack. Cool completely, about 30 minutes.

3 In medium bowl, beat all frosting ingredients except malted milk balls on medium speed until smooth. Frost cupcakes. Sprinkle with 1⅔ cups malted milk balls.

1 Cupcake: Calories 240 (Calories from Fat 90); Total Fat 10g (Saturated Fat 4.5g); Cholesterol 30mg; Sodium 190mg; Total Carbohydrate 37g (Dietary Fiber 0g); Protein 2g

Nutty Chocolate Chip Picnic Cake

Prep Time: 15 min   Start to Finish: 1 hr 50 min   15 Servings

½ cup miniature semisweet chocolate chips
⅓ cup packed brown sugar
⅓ cup chopped pecans
1 box devil's food cake mix
Water, oil and eggs called for on cake mix box

1 Heat oven to 350°F. Lightly grease bottom only of 13×9-inch pan with shortening or cooking spray.

2 In small bowl, mix chocolate chips, brown sugar and pecans; set aside. Make cake mix as directed on box, using water, oil and eggs. Pour into pan. Sprinkle with chocolate chip mixture.

3 Bake 30 to 35 minutes or until toothpick inserted in center comes out clean. Cool completely, about 1 hour. Store tightly covered.

For an extra dose of decadence, drizzle the cake with caramel or hot fudge topping. Or decorate with your favorite frosting.

1 Serving: Calories 290 (Calories from Fat 130); Total Fat 14g (Saturated Fat 3.5g); Cholesterol 40mg; Sodium 280mg; Total Carbohydrate 37g (Dietary Fiber 2g); Protein 3g

Italian Sausage Burgers

Backyard Beer Burgers

Veggie Burger and Grilled Pepper Sandwiches

Summertime Mushroom-Tomato Kabobs

Greek Pork Kabobs

Buffalo Chicken Kabobs

Jerk Shrimp Kabobs

Summer Herb Steaks

Grilled Jerk Flank Steak

Chipotle Salsa Ribs

Apple-Maple Brined Pork Tenderloin

Fiery Pork Tenderloin with Pineapple Salsa

Hoisin-Glazed Pork Chops

Southwestern Pork Chops

Chicken with Oregano-Peach Sauce

Three-Herb Chicken

Lemon Chicken with Grilled Fennel and Onions

Ginger-Lime Tuna Steaks

Dill Salmon

Grilled Salmon with Fresh Lime Cream

3

great for the grill

Italian Sausage Burgers

Prep Time: 10 min ∎ Start to Finish: 25 min ∎ 6 Sandwiches

1 lb lean ground beef
½ lb bulk mild or hot Italian sausage
2 tablespoons Italian-style bread crumbs
6 slices (¾ oz each) mozzarella cheese
12 slices Italian bread, ½ inch thick
½ cup sun-dried tomato mayonnaise
1 cup shredded lettuce
1 medium tomato, thinly sliced

1 Heat coals or gas grill for direct heat. In large bowl, mix beef, sausage and bread crumbs. Shape mixture into 6 patties, about ½ inch thick and 3½ inches in diameter.

2 Cover and grill patties 4 to 6 inches from medium heat 12 to 15 minutes, turning once, until meat thermometer inserted in center reads 160°F. Top patties with cheese. Cover and grill about 1 minute longer or until cheese is melted. Add bread slices to side of grill for last 2 to 3 minutes of grilling, turning once, until lightly toasted.

3 Spread toasted bread with mayonnaise; top 6 bread slices with lettuce, tomato and patties. Top with remaining bread slices.

You can make your own sun-dried tomato mayonnaise by combining ⅓ cup mayonnaise with about 2 tablespoons chopped sun-dried tomatoes. Plain mayonnaise works fine here, too.

1 Sandwich: Calories 490 (Calories from Fat 280); Total Fat 31g (Saturated Fat 10g); Cholesterol 85mg; Sodium 750mg; Total Carbohydrate 25g (Dietary Fiber 2g); Protein 29g

Backyard Beer Burgers

Prep Time: 10 min ■ Start to Finish: 25 min ■ 6 Sandwiches

1½ lb ground beef
1 small onion, finely chopped (¼ cup)
¼ cup regular or nonalcoholic beer
1 tablespoon Worcestershire sauce
1 teaspoon salt
¼ teaspoon pepper
2 cloves garlic, finely chopped
6 rye or whole wheat hamburger buns, split
Ketchup, if desired
Pickle planks, if desired

1 Heat coals or gas grill for direct heat. Mix all ingredients except buns, ketchup and pickles. Shape mixture into 6 patties, about ¾ inch thick.

2 Grill patties uncovered about 4 inches from medium heat 10 to 15 minutes, turning once, until no longer pink in center and juice is clear. Add buns, cut sides down, for last 4 minutes of grilling or until toasted.

3 Top burgers with ketchup and pickle planks; serve on buns.

Don't be tempted to press down on the hamburgers with a spatula while they're cooking, or you'll squeeze out the flavorful juices! Using a meat thermometer will ensure that you cook grilled foods to the correct temperature before serving. Ground beef patties should reach 160°F to be thoroughly cooked.

1 Sandwich: Calories 320 (Calories from Fat 130); Total Fat 14g (Saturated Fat 5g); Cholesterol 70mg; Sodium 620mg; Total Carbohydrate 24g (Dietary Fiber 2g); Protein 24g

Veggie Burger and Grilled Pepper Sandwiches

Prep Time: 10 min ■ Start to Finish: 25 min ■ 4 Sandwiches

4 frozen soy-protein burgers
½ teaspoon salt
4 slices (¾ oz each) mozzarella cheese
4 whole-grain sandwich buns, split
¼ cup roasted-garlic mayonnaise
1 cup roasted bell peppers
1 medium tomato, sliced

1 Heat coals or gas grill for direct heat. Sprinkle burgers with salt.

2 Cover and grill burgers 4 to 6 inches from medium heat 8 to 10 minutes, turning once or twice, until thoroughly heated. Top each burger with cheese. Cover and grill about 1 minute or just until cheese is melted.

3 Spread cut sides of buns with garlic mayonnaise. Thinly slice bell peppers. Layer tomato, burger and bell peppers on each bun.

1 Sandwich: Calories 450 (Calories from Fat 210); Total Fat 24g (Saturated Fat 6g); Cholesterol 20mg; Sodium 1190mg; Total Carbohydrate 38g (Dietary Fiber 4g); Protein 21g

Summertime Mushroom-Tomato Kabobs

Prep Time: 15 min ▪ Start to Finish: 25 min ▪ 4 Kabobs

4 fresh portabella mushroom caps (about 3 oz each)
6 red cherry or miniature plum (Roma) tomatoes
6 yellow cherry tomatoes
6 medium green onions, cut into 2-inch pieces
¼ cup red wine vinaigrette or Greek vinaigrette dressing

1 Heat coals or gas grill for direct heat. Scrape underside of mushroom caps, using small spoon, to remove dark gills and stems. Cut each cap into 6 pieces.

2 Thread mushroom pieces, red and yellow tomatoes and onion pieces alternately on each of four 14- to 15-inch metal skewers.

3 Cover and grill kabobs 4 to 6 inches from medium heat 8 to 10 minutes, turning and brushing with vinaigrette occasionally, until mushrooms are tender. Place on serving plate. Drizzle with any remaining dressing.

When threading the veggies on the skewers, leave about a ¼-inch space between the pieces so they cook evenly.

1 Kabob: Calories 110 (Calories from Fat 60); Total Fat 7g (Saturated Fat 0.5g); Cholesterol 0mg; Sodium 140mg; Total Carbohydrate 9g (Dietary Fiber 2g); Protein 4g

Greek Pork Kabobs

Prep Time: 15 min ■ Start to Finish: 30 min ■ 4 Servings

½ cup Greek vinaigrette dressing
1 tablespoon chopped fresh parsley
1 lb boneless pork loin, cut into 1-inch cubes
1 red onion, cut into 8 wedges
1 large red or green bell pepper, cut into 8 pieces

1 Heat coals or gas grill for direct heat. In large bowl, mix dressing and parsley; stir in pork, onion and bell pepper. Thread pork, onion and bell pepper alternately on each of four 15-inch metal skewers, leaving ¼-inch space between each piece. Reserve remaining vinaigrette in bowl.

2 Cover and grill kabobs 4 to 6 inches from medium heat 10 to 15 minutes, turning kabobs 2 or 3 times and brushing with vinaigrette during last 5 minutes of grilling, until pork is no longer pink in center. Discard any remaining vinaigrette.

Skewers with flat sides (rather than round) hold ingredients more securely and keep pieces in place when you turn the kabobs.

1 Serving: Calories 300 (Calories from Fat 150); Total Fat 17g (Saturated Fat 3.5g); Cholesterol 75mg; Sodium 280mg; Total Carbohydrate 9g (Dietary Fiber 1g); Protein 26g

Buffalo Chicken Kabobs

Prep Time: 20 min ∎ Start to Finish: 40 min ∎ 4 Servings

1 lb boneless, skinless chicken breasts, cut into 24 cubes
24 (about 1 ½ cups) refrigerated new potato wedges (from 1-lb 4-oz bag)
24 pieces (about 1 inch) celery
2 tablespoons olive or vegetable oil
1 teaspoon red pepper sauce
½ teaspoon black and red pepper blend
½ teaspoon seasoned salt
6 cups torn romaine lettuce
½ cup shredded carrot
½ cup blue cheese dressing

1 Heat coals or gas grill for direct heat. Thread chicken, potatoes and celery alternately on each of eight 8- to 10-inch metal skewers, leaving ¼-inch space between each piece. Mix oil and pepper sauce; brush over chicken and vegetables. Sprinkle with pepper blend and seasoned salt.

2 Cover and grill kabobs 4 to 6 inches from medium heat 15 to 20 minutes, turning occasionally, until chicken is no longer pink in center and potatoes are tender.

3 Arrange romaine and carrot on 4 individual serving plates. Top each with 2 kabobs. Serve with dressing.

This is a super one-dish entrée salad, so all you need to add is warm garlic bread. Wrap the bread in foil, then heat it on the grill for 5 to 10 minutes.

1 Serving: Calories 430 (Calories from Fat 210); Total Fat 24g (Saturated Fat 3g); Cholesterol 75mg; Sodium 590mg; Total Carbohydrate 26g (Dietary Fiber 5g); Protein 29g

Jerk Shrimp Kabobs

Prep Time: 20 min ∎ Start to Finish: 35 min ∎ 4 Kabobs

2 tablespoons olive or vegetable oil
2 teaspoons Caribbean jerk seasoning (dry)
¼ teaspoon salt
1 ½ lb uncooked peeled deveined large shrimp (21 to 30) or extra-large shrimp
    (16 to 20), thawed if frozen, tail shells removed
16 chunks (about 1 inch) fresh pineapple
1 red bell pepper, cut into 16 pieces
¼ cup pineapple preserves
2 tablespoons lime juice

1 Heat coals or gas grill for direct heat. In large bowl, mix oil, jerk seasoning and salt. Add shrimp, pineapple and bell pepper; toss to coat. Thread shrimp, pineapple and bell pepper alternately on each of four 12- to 15-inch metal skewers, leaving ¼-inch space between each piece. Mix preserves and lime juice; set aside.

2 Cover and grill kabobs 4 to 6 inches from medium heat 4 minutes. Turn kabobs; brush with preserves mixture. Cover and grill 4 to 8 minutes longer or until shrimp are pink and firm.

Although the ingredients in Caribbean jerk seasoning vary, the most common combination is a blend of chiles, thyme, sweet spices, garlic and onions. Traditionally, jerk seasoning is used to flavor grilled meats.

1 Kabob: Calories 250 (Calories from Fat 60); Total Fat 7g (Saturated Fat 1g); Cholesterol 240mg; Sodium 430mg; Total Carbohydrate 22g (Dietary Fiber 2g); Protein 27g

Summer Herb Steaks

Prep Time: 25 min ▪ Start to Finish: 35 min ▪ 4 Servings

¼ cup Dijon mustard
2 teaspoons chopped fresh or ½ teaspoon dried rosemary leaves, crumbled
1 teaspoon coarsely ground pepper
2 cloves garlic, finely chopped
4 beef top loin steaks, about 1 inch thick (about 1 lb)

1 Heat coals or gas grill for direct heat. In small bowl, mix mustard, rosemary, pepper and garlic; spread on both sides of beef.

2 Cover and grill beef over medium heat 1 minute on each side to seal in juices. Cover and grill 8 to 9 minutes longer for medium doneness, turning once.

Top loin is one of the lower-fat cuts of beef. Other "skinny" cuts include eye round, top round, round tip, tenderloin and sirloin.

1 Serving: Calories 190 (Calories from Fat 80); Total Fat 9g (Saturated Fat 3g); Cholesterol 65mg; Sodium 430mg; Total Carbohydrate 2g (Dietary Fiber 0g); Protein 25g

Grilled Jerk Flank Steak

Prep Time: 15 min ▪ Start to Finish: 4 hrs 30 min ▪ 6 Servings

3 tablespoons teriyaki marinade and sauce (from 10-oz bottle)
1 tablespoon canola or vegetable oil
2 teaspoons pumpkin pie spice
½ teaspoon dried thyme leaves
½ teaspoon salt
¼ teaspoon pepper
2 cloves garlic, finely chopped
1 jalapeño chile with seeds, finely chopped
1½ lb beef flank steak

1 Place all ingredients except beef in heavy-duty resealable plastic food-storage bag. Add beef steak; seal bag and turn to coat beef. Refrigerate at least 4 hours but no longer than 24 hours.

2 Heat coals or gas grill for direct heat. Remove beef from marinade; discard marinade.

3 Cover and grill beef 4 to 5 inches from hot heat about 10 minutes, turning once, until slightly pink when cut in center. Let stand 5 minutes. To serve, cut across grain into thin slices.

To broil: Place marinated steak on broiler pan. Broil with top 4 to 5 inches from heat using times in recipe as a guide, turning once.

Pumpkin pie spice is a combination of cinnamon, nutmeg, cloves, ginger and sometimes mace—all common spices in Caribbean cooking.

1 Serving: Calories 180 (Calories from Fat 80); Total Fat 9g (Saturated Fat 3g); Cholesterol 65mg; Sodium 240mg; Total Carbohydrate 0g (Dietary Fiber 0g); Protein 25g

Chipotle Salsa Ribs

Prep Time: 10 min ▪ Start to Finish: 6 hrs 10 min ▪ 6 Servings

Southwestern Rub

1 tablespoon packed brown sugar
1 teaspoon chili powder
1 teaspoon paprika
½ teaspoon ground cumin
½ teaspoon seasoned salt
½ teaspoon garlic-pepper blend
¼ teaspoon ground ginger

Ribs

4 lb pork loin back ribs (not cut into serving pieces)
½ cup chipotle salsa
¼ cup chili sauce
2 tablespoons orange marmalade

1 In small bowl, prepare rub by mixing all ingredients. Rub mixture over ribs. Wrap tightly in plastic wrap and refrigerate at least 4 hours but no longer than 12 hours.

2 If using charcoal grill, place drip pan directly under grilling area, and arrange coals around edge of firebox. Heat coals or gas grill for indirect heat. Cover and grill ribs over drip pan or over unheated side of gas grill and 4 to 6 inches from medium heat 1 hour 30 minutes to 2 hours, turning occasionally, until tender.

3 In small bowl, mix salsa, chili sauce and marmalade. Brush over ribs during last 10 to 15 minutes of grilling. Heat remaining salsa mixture to boiling; boil and stir 1 minute. Cut ribs into serving-size pieces. Serve salsa mixture with ribs.

1 Serving: Calories 610 (Calories from Fat 400); Total Fat 44g (Saturated Fat 16g); Cholesterol 175mg; Sodium 500mg; Total Carbohydrate 11g (Dietary Fiber 1g); Protein 43g

When food is cooked away from the heat source, it's called "indirect-heat" grilling. This is the best way to cook large cuts or long-cooking foods because the indirect heat won't burn or overcook the food.

Apple-Maple Brined Pork Tenderloin

Prep Time: 15 min ■ Start to Finish: 8 hrs 40 min ■ 6 Servings

4 cups cold water
2 cups apple cider
½ cup maple-flavored or real maple syrup
¼ cup salt
2 pork tenderloins (about 1 lb each)
1 tablespoon chopped fresh rosemary leaves
½ teaspoon coarsely ground pepper
¼ teaspoon garlic powder

1 In large container or stockpot, stir water, cider, maple syrup and salt until salt is dissolved. Add pork to brine mixture. Cover and refrigerate at least 8 hours but no longer than 12 hours.

2 Heat coals or gas grill for direct heat. Remove pork from brine mixture; rinse thoroughly under cool running water and pat dry. Discard brine. Sprinkle pork with rosemary, pepper and garlic powder.

3 Cover and grill pork 4 to 6 inches from medium heat 20 to 25 minutes, turning occasionally, until pork has slight blush of pink in center and meat thermometer inserted in center reads 160°F.

Brining is an age-old process for preserving meats. Today, this simple method of soaking meat in a saltwater solution makes it exceptionally moist, juicy and flavorful.

1 Serving: Calories 190 (Calories from Fat 50); Total Fat 6g (Saturated Fat 2g); Cholesterol 95mg; Sodium 460mg; Total Carbohydrate 2g (Dietary Fiber 0g); Protein 34g

Fiery Pork Tenderloin with Pineapple Salsa

Prep Time: 40 min ■ Start to Finish: 40 min ■ 4 Servings

Pork

2 teaspoons canola or soybean oil

2 pork tenderloins (¾ lb each)

1 teaspoon black pepper

¼ to ½ teaspoon ground red pepper (cayenne)

½ teaspoon salt

Pineapple Salsa

1 can (8 oz) pineapple tidbits, drained

4 medium green onions, sliced (¼ cup)

¼ cup chopped red bell pepper

2 tablespoons chopped fresh or 2 teaspoons dried mint leaves

½ teaspoon grated lime peel

2 teaspoons lime juice

¼ teaspoon salt

1 Brush grill rack with oil. Heat coals or gas grill for direct heat. Rub 1 teaspoon oil onto each pork tenderloin; sprinkle with peppers and ½ teaspoon salt.

2 Cover and grill pork over medium heat 20 to 30 minutes, turning 3 times, until pork has slight blush of pink in center and meat thermometer inserted in center reads 160°F.

3 Meanwhile, in medium bowl, mix all salsa ingredients. Cut pork into ½-inch slices. Serve with salsa.

Serve fresh green beans, roasted or steamed, as an easy, healthy side dish.

1 Serving: Calories 270 (Calories from Fat 80); Total Fat 9g (Saturated Fat 2.5g); Cholesterol 110mg; Sodium 520mg; Total Carbohydrate 10g (Dietary Fiber 1g); Protein 39g

Hoisin-Glazed Pork Chops

Prep Time: 10 min ∎ Start to Finish: 25 min ∎ 4 Servings

½ cup barbecue sauce
¼ cup hoisin sauce
2 tablespoons dry sherry, if desired
1 tablespoon honey
4 boneless pork loin chops, about ½ inch thick (about 1 lb)
½ teaspoon garlic-pepper blend
¼ teaspoon salt
¼ teaspoon ground ginger

1 Heat coals or gas grill for direct heat. In 1-quart saucepan, mix barbecue sauce, hoisin sauce, sherry and honey. Cook over medium heat about 5 minutes, stirring occasionally, until flavors are blended.

2 Sprinkle pork with garlic pepper, salt and ginger. Cover and grill pork 4 to 6 inches from medium heat 10 to 12 minutes, turning frequently and brushing with hoisin glaze during last 5 minutes of grilling, until pork is no longer pink in center.

3 Heat remaining glaze to boiling; boil and stir 1 minute. Serve pork with remaining glaze.

Hoisin is a thick, reddish brown sauce with a spicy-sweet flavor that's often used in Chinese cooking. It's a blend of soybeans, garlic, chiles and spices. Look for it in the ethnic-foods section of the grocery store.

1 Serving: Calories 260 (Calories from Fat 80); Total Fat 9g (Saturated Fat 3g); Cholesterol 65mg; Sodium 760mg; Total Carbohydrate 22g (Dietary Fiber 0g); Protein 24g

Southwestern Pork Chops

Prep Time: 10 min ■ Start to Finish: 1 hr 20 min ■ 8 Servings

8 pork loin or rib chops, about ½ inch thick (about 2 lb)
1 tablespoon chili powder
1 teaspoon ground cumin
¼ teaspoon ground red pepper (cayenne)
¼ teaspoon salt
1 large clove garlic, finely chopped

1 Trim excess fat from pork. In small bowl, mix remaining ingredients; rub evenly on both sides of pork. Cover and refrigerate 1 hour to blend flavors.

2 Heat coals or gas grill for direct heat. Cover and grill pork 4 to 6 inches from medium heat 8 to 10 minutes, turning frequently, until no longer pink when cut near bone.

To keep food from sticking and to make cleanup a breeze, brush the grill rack with vegetable oil or spray with cooking spray before heating the grill.

1 Serving: Calories 170 (Calories from Fat 70); Total Fat 8g (Saturated Fat 3g); Cholesterol 65mg; Sodium 125mg; Total Carbohydrate 0g (Dietary Fiber 0g); Protein 23g

Chicken with Oregano-Peach Sauce

Prep Time: 15 min ▪ Start to Finish: 35 min ▪ 4 Servings

½ cup peach preserves
¼ cup raspberry vinegar
2 tablespoons chopped fresh oregano leaves
4 boneless, skinless chicken breast halves (1¼ lb)
½ teaspoon garlic-pepper blend
½ teaspoon seasoned salt

1 Heat coals or gas grill for direct heat. In 1-quart saucepan, heat preserves and vinegar to boiling, stirring constantly, until preserves are melted. Spoon about ¼ cup mixture into small bowl or custard cup for brushing on chicken. Stir oregano into remaining mixture and reserve to serve with chicken.

2 Sprinkle chicken with garlic pepper and seasoned salt.

3 Cover and grill chicken 4 to 6 inches from medium heat 15 to 20 minutes, turning once and brushing with preserves mixture during last 10 minutes of grilling, until juice of chicken is no longer pink when centers of thickest pieces are cut. Discard any remaining preserves mixture brushed on chicken. Serve chicken with reserved preserves mixture with oregano.

When buying fresh oregano, look for bright-green bunches with no sign of wilting or yellowing. Store it in the refrigerator in a plastic bag for up to three days.

1 Serving: Calories 220 (Calories from Fat 35); Total Fat 4g (Saturated Fat 1g); Cholesterol 75mg; Sodium 250mg; Total Carbohydrate 19g (Dietary Fiber 0g); Protein 27g

Three-Herb Chicken

Prep Time: 10 min ■ Start to Finish: 1 hr 25 min ■ 4 Servings

Herb Marinade
½ cup vegetable oil
½ cup lime juice
2 tablespoons chopped fresh or 2 teaspoons dried basil leaves
2 tablespoons chopped fresh or 2 teaspoons dried oregano leaves
2 tablespoons chopped fresh or 2 teaspoons dried thyme leaves
1 teaspoon onion powder
¼ teaspoon lemon-pepper seasoning

Chicken
4 chicken thighs (about 1 lb)
4 chicken drumsticks (about 1 lb)

1 Prepare marinade by mixing all ingredients in shallow glass, plastic dish or resealable plastic food storage bag. Add chicken thighs and drumsticks to marinade; turn to coat. Cover dish or seal bag and refrigerate, turning chicken occasionally, at least 30 minutes but no longer than 24 hours.

2 Heat coals or gas grill for direct heat. Remove chicken from marinade; reserve marinade. Cover and grill chicken, skin sides down, 5 to 6 inches from medium heat 8 to 10 minutes. Turn chicken; brush with marinade. Cover and grill 25 to 35 minutes longer, turning occasionally and brushing with marinade, until juice of chicken is no longer pink when centers of thickest pieces are cut. Discard any remaining marinade.

1 Serving: Calories 430 (Calories from Fat 300); Total Fat 33g (Saturated Fat 7g); Cholesterol 100mg; Sodium 95mg; Total Carbohydrate 1g (Dietary Fiber 0g); Protein 31g

Lemon Chicken with Grilled Fennel and Onions

Prep Time: 40 min ▪ Start to Finish: 55 min ▪ 6 Servings

6 bone-in chicken breasts (about 3 lb)
¼ cup olive or vegetable oil
1 teaspoon grated lemon peel
¼ cup lemon juice
2 tablespoons chopped fresh or 2 teaspoons dried oregano leaves
½ teaspoon salt
2 medium fennel bulbs, cut into ½-inch slices
1 medium red onion, cut into ½-inch slices

1 Place chicken in shallow glass or plastic dish. In small bowl, mix oil, lemon peel, lemon juice, oregano and salt; pour over chicken. Cover and let stand 15 minutes.

2 Heat coals or gas grill for direct heat. Remove chicken from marinade; reserve marinade. Brush fennel and onion with marinade.

3 Cover and grill chicken (skin sides down), fennel and onion over medium heat 15 to 20 minutes, turning once and brushing frequently with marinade, until juice of chicken is no longer pink when centers of thickest pieces are cut. Discard any remaining marinade.

For an easy summer meal, serve this lemony chicken with fresh tomato slices and angel hair pasta.

1 Serving: Calories 240 (Calories from Fat 100); Total Fat 11g (Saturated Fat 2g); Cholesterol 75mg; Sodium 310mg; Total Carbohydrate 8g (Dietary Fiber 3g); Protein 28g

Ginger-Lime Tuna Steaks

Prep Time: 10 min ■ Start to Finish: 1 hr 25 min ■ 4 Servings

1½ lb tuna steaks, ¾ to 1 inch thick
¼ cup lime juice
2 tablespoons olive or vegetable oil
2 teaspoons finely chopped gingerroot
½ teaspoon salt
⅛ teaspoon ground red pepper (cayenne)
2 cloves garlic, crushed
Lime wedges, if desired

1 If fish steaks are large, cut into 6 serving pieces. In shallow glass or plastic dish or resealable plastic food-storage bag, mix remaining ingredients except lime wedges. Add fish; turn to coat. Cover dish or seal bag and refrigerate, turning fish once, at least 1 hour but no longer than 24 hours.

2 Heat coals or gas grill for direct heat. Remove fish from marinade; reserve marinade. Cover and grill fish about 4 inches from medium heat 11 to 15 minutes, brushing 2 or 3 times with marinade and turning once, until fish flakes easily with fork and is slightly pink in center. Discard any remaining marinade. Serve fish with lime wedges.

For variety, try this recipe using swordfish or halibut steaks instead of the tuna steaks.

1 Serving: Calories 280 (Calories from Fat 120); Total Fat 13g (Saturated Fat 3g); Cholesterol 65mg; Sodium 270mg; Total Carbohydrate 0g (Dietary Fiber 0g); Protein 40g

Dill Salmon

Prep Time: 10 min ■ Start to Finish: 40 min ■ 6 Servings

1 large salmon fillet (about 2 lbs)
1 tablespoon vegetable oil
¼ teaspoon pepper
½ cup dill dip
2 tablespoons milk

1 Heat coals or gas grill for direct heat. Place fish on 24-inch piece of heavy-duty foil. Brush fish with oil; sprinkle with pepper. Wrap foil securely around fish.

2 Cover and grill fish 4 to 6 inches from medium heat 20 to 30 minutes or until fish flakes easily with fork.

3 Mix dill dip with milk until smooth. Serve salmon with dill sauce.

For the safest possible picnic, remember that perishable food should be consumed within two hours (or one hour if the outside temperature is over 90°F).

1 Serving: Calories 270 (Calories from Fat 140); Total Fat 15g (Saturated Fat 3.5g); Cholesterol 90mg; Sodium 210mg; Total Carbohydrate 1g (Dietary Fiber 0g); Protein 31g

Grilled Salmon with Fresh Lime Cream

Prep Time: 30 min ▪ Start to Finish: 1 hr 5 min ▪ 6 Servings

Salmon
1 teaspoon grated lime peel
¼ cup lime juice
2 tablespoons honey
1 tablespoon chopped fresh or 1 teaspoon dried dill weed
2 teaspoons canola or soybean oil
1¼ lb salmon fillets, cut into 6 serving pieces
½ teaspoon salt

Lime Cream
⅓ cup fat-free mayonnaise
1 teaspoon grated lime peel
2 teaspoons lime juice

1 In small bowl, mix 1 teaspoon lime peel, ¼ cup lime juice, honey, dill weed and oil.

2 In 8-inch square (2-quart) glass baking dish, arrange salmon pieces, skin sides up, in single layer. Pour marinade over salmon; turn in marinade to cover all sides. Cover with plastic wrap and refrigerate 20 to 30 minutes.

3 Brush grill rack with oil. Heat coals or gas grill for direct heat. Remove salmon from marinade; discard marinade. Sprinkle salmon with salt. Place skin sides down on grill. Cover and grill over medium heat 10 to 15 minutes or until salmon flakes easily with fork.

4 Meanwhile, in small bowl, mix all lime cream ingredients with wire whisk. Serve with salmon.

1 Serving: Calories 180 (Calories from Fat 70); Total Fat 7g (Saturated Fat 2g); Cholesterol 75mg; Sodium 370mg; Total Carbohydrate 4g (Dietary Fiber 0g); Protein 24g

Neptune Pasta Salad

Roasted Sweet Pepper Pasta Salad
with Herbs and Feta

Mediterranean Quinoa Salad

Confetti Rice

Black Bean Chili Salad

Fiesta Taco Salad with Beans

Grilled Potato Wedges with
Barbeque Dipping Sauce

Caesar and Bacon Potato Salad

Garlic Oven Fries

Easy Grilled Vegetables

Grilled Corn with Chile-Lime Spread

Portabella Mushrooms with Herbs

Dilled Cucumber-Tomato Salad

Lime-Mint Melon Salad

Asian Slaw

Tortellini, Brocoli and Bacon Salad

Picnic Pasta Salad

Mediterranean Potato Salad

Smoked Sausage Baked Beans

California Citrus Broccoli Slaw

4

sumptuous
sides

Neptune Pasta Salad

Prep Time: 25 min   Start to Finish: 25 min   4 Servings

1 box Caesar pasta salad mix
¼ cup cold water
3 tablespoons vegetable oil
1 package (8 oz) refrigerated flake-style imitation crabmeat
1½ cups broccoli florets

1 Fill 3-quart or larger saucepan ⅔ full of water. Heat to boiling. Add contents of pasta pouch to boiling water. Gently boil about 12 minutes, stirring occasionally, until pasta is tender; drain. Rinse with cold water until chilled; drain.

2 In large bowl, mix seasoning mix, water and oil. Stir in pasta mixture, imitation crabmeat and broccoli. Toss with croutons and parmesan topping just before serving.

Add 1 cup cherry tomato halves for a burst of color and vine-ripe flavor!

1 Serving: Calories 350 (Calories from Fat 110); Total Fat 12g (Saturated Fat 1.5g); Cholesterol 15mg; Sodium 1220mg; Total Carbohydrate 43g (Dietary Fiber 2g); Protein 16g

Roasted Sweet Pepper Pasta Salad with Herbs and Feta

Prep Time: 35 min   Start to Finish: 35 min   8 Servings (1¼ cups each)

2 large red or yellow bell peppers, cut into 1-inch pieces
1 medium red onion, cut into wedges (about 2 cups)
Cooking spray
3 cups uncooked penne pasta (10 oz)
1 cup sliced 70%-less-fat turkey pepperoni (about 3 oz), cut in half
½ cup crumbled feta cheese
½ cup fat-free Italian dressing
2 tablespoons chopped fresh basil leaves
1 tablespoon chopped fresh mint leaves

1 Heat oven to 450°F. Spray 13×9×2-inch pan with cooking spray. Place bell peppers and onion in single layer in pan. Spray vegetables with cooking spray. Bake uncovered 15 to 20 minutes or until vegetables are lightly browned and tender.

2 Meanwhile, cook and drain pasta as directed on package. Rinse with cold water; drain.

3 In large bowl, toss bell peppers, onion, pasta and remaining ingredients. Serve immediately, or refrigerate 1 to 2 hours.

1 Serving: Calories 220 (Calories from Fat 45); Total Fat 5g (Saturated Fat 2g); Cholesterol 20mg; Sodium 540mg; Total Carbohydrate 33g (Dietary Fiber 3g); Protein 10g

Mediterranean Quinoa Salad

Prep Time: 30 min   Start to Finish: 1 hr 35 min   4 Servings

1 cup uncooked quinoa
2 cups roasted garlic-seasoned chicken broth (from two 14-oz cans)
½ cup chopped drained roasted red bell peppers (from 7-oz jar)
½ cup cubed provolone cheese
¼ cup chopped kalamata olives
2 tablespoons chopped fresh basil leaves
2 tablespoons fat-free Italian dressing

1 Rinse quinoa under cold water 1 minute; drain.

2 In 2-quart saucepan, heat quinoa and broth to boiling; reduce heat. Cover and simmer 15 to 20 minutes or until quinoa is tender; drain. Cool completely, about 45 minutes.

3 In large serving bowl, toss quinoa and remaining ingredients. Serve immediately, or refrigerate 1 to 2 hours before serving.

Quinoa is a popular grain in South American cuisine and is gaining popularity in the United States.

1 Serving: Calories 260 (Calories from Fat 80); Total Fat 9g (Saturated Fat 3.5g); Cholesterol 10mg; Sodium 820mg; Total Carbohydrate 33g (Dietary Fiber 3g); Protein 13g

Confetti Rice

Prep Time: 10 min   Start to Finish: 30 min   8 Servings (½ cup each)

1¼ cups water
1 can (14 oz) 33%-less-sodium chicken broth
1 teaspoon salt-free seasoning blend
1 cup uncooked converted rice
1 cup chopped broccoli
½ cup shredded carrot (about 1 medium)
1 jar (2 oz) diced pimientos, drained

1 In 3-quart saucepan, heat water, broth and seasoning blend to boiling. Stir in rice; reduce heat to low. Cover and simmer 15 minutes.

2 Stir in broccoli and carrot. Cover and cook about 5 minutes or until rice and broccoli are tender. Stir in pimientos. Let stand 5 minutes.

Frozen cut broccoli can be substituted for the fresh. Just be sure to chop up any large pieces.

1 Serving: Calories 100 (Calories from Fat 5); Total Fat 0.5g (Saturated Fat 0g); Cholesterol 0mg; Sodium 115mg; Total Carbohydrate 22g (Dietary Fiber 0g); Protein 3g

Black Bean Chili Salad

Prep Time: 10 min   Start to Finish: 10 min   4 Servings

Chili Vinaigrette Dressing
¼ cup red wine vinegar
2 tablespoons vegetable oil
½ teaspoon chili powder
¼ teaspoon ground cumin
1 small clove garlic, finely chopped

Salad
1 cup frozen whole kernel corn (from 1-lb bag), thawed, drained
1 cup diced jicama
1 medium tomato, seeded, chopped (¾ cup)
2 medium green onions, sliced (2 tablespoons)
2 cans (15 oz each) black beans, rinsed, drained

1 In large glass or plastic bowl, mix all dressing ingredients.

2 Stir in all salad ingredients.

1 Serving: Calories 390 (Calories from Fat 70); Total Fat 8g (Saturated Fat 1.5g); Cholesterol 0mg; Sodium 10mg; Total Carbohydrate 62g (Dietary Fiber 15g); Protein 18g

Fiesta Taco Salad with Beans

Prep Time: 15 min   Start to Finish: 20 min   5 Servings (2 cups each)

1 can (15 oz) black beans, rinsed, drained
½ cup taco sauce
6 cups lettuce, torn into bite-size pieces
1 medium green bell pepper, cut into strips
2 medium tomatoes, cut into wedges
½ cup pitted ripe olives, drained
1 cup corn chips
1 cup shredded Cheddar cheese (4 oz)
½ cup reduced-fat Thousand Island dressing

1 In 2-quart saucepan, cook beans and taco sauce over medium heat 4 to 5 minutes, stirring occasionally, until thoroughly heated.

2 In large bowl, toss lettuce, bell pepper, tomatoes, olives and corn chips. Spoon bean mixture over lettuce mixture; toss. Sprinkle with cheese. Serve immediately with dressing.

You can cut back on the fat and calories in this recipe by using reduced-fat Cheddar cheese and fat-free Thousand Island dressing.

1 Serving: Calories 350 (Calories from Fat 130); Total Fat 15g (Saturated Fat 6g); Cholesterol 25mg; Sodium 980mg; Total Carbohydrate 40g (Dietary Fiber 8g); Protein 15g

Grilled Potato Wedges with Barbecue Dipping Sauce

Prep Time: 45 min   Start to Finish: 45 min   4 Servings

4 medium white potatoes
Cooking spray
1 teaspoon Cajun seasoning
½ cup reduced-fat sour cream
2 tablespoons barbecue sauce

1 Heat coals or gas grill for direct heat. Cut each potato lengthwise into 8 wedges; pat dry with paper towels. Spray potato wedges thoroughly with cooking spray. Sprinkle with Cajun seasoning. Place in grill basket (grill "wok").

2 Cover and grill potato wedges over medium heat 30 to 40 minutes, stirring every 10 minutes, until tender.

3 In small bowl, mix sour cream and barbecue sauce. Serve with potato wedges.

If Cajun seasoning isn't available, make your own seasoning, using ½ teaspoon chili powder, ¼ teaspoon ground oregano and ¼ teaspoon onion or garlic salt.

1 Serving: Calories 160 (Calories from Fat 40); Total Fat 4g (Saturated Fat 2.5g); Cholesterol 10mg; Sodium 240mg; Total Carbohydrate 30g (Dietary Fiber 3g); Protein 4g

Caesar and Bacon Potato Salad

Prep Time: 35 min   Start to Finish: 1 hr 50 min   6 Servings

6 unpeeled small red potatoes, cut into ½-inch cubes (3 cups)
1 cup frozen cut green beans (from 1-lb bag)
2 hard-cooked eggs
½ cup Caesar dressing
2 tablespoons chopped fresh basil leaves
½ teaspoon salt
⅛ teaspoon coarse pepper
4 slices cooked bacon, chopped
2 cups romaine lettuce, torn into bite-size pieces
Additional chopped fresh basil leaves, if desired

1 In 2-quart saucepan, place potatoes; add enough water to cover potatoes. Heat to boiling; reduce heat to medium. Cook 5 minutes. Add green beans. Cook 4 to 6 minutes or until potatoes and beans are tender; drain. Cool 15 minutes. Peel and chop one of the eggs.

2 In medium bowl, mix dressing, 2 tablespoons basil, salt and pepper. Add potatoes, beans, chopped egg and bacon; stir gently to mix. Cover and refrigerate 1 hour.

3 Line serving plate with lettuce. Spoon salad onto lettuce. Peel and coarsely chop remaining egg; sprinkle over salad. Garnish with additional basil.

1 Serving: Calories 220 (Calories from Fat 140); Total Fat 16g (Saturated Fat 3g); Cholesterol 75mg; Sodium 520mg; Total Carbohydrate 16g (Dietary Fiber 3g); Protein 6g

Garlic Oven Fries

Prep Time: 10 min   Start to Finish: 30 min   4 Servings

4 medium red potatoes (2½ to 3 inch), each cut in 8 wedges
2 teaspoons olive or vegetable oil
1 teaspoon dried basil leaves
1 teaspoon garlic salt

1 Heat oven to 500°F. Spray 15×10×1-inch pan with cooking spray. In medium bowl, toss potatoes with oil to coat. Sprinkle with basil and garlic salt. Arrange in single layer in baking pan.

2 Bake uncovered 15 to 18 minutes, stirring once, until potatoes are tender but crisp on outside.

Red potatoes have a slightly waxy texture and retain their shape better when cooked than russet potatoes do.

1 Serving: Calories 130 (Calories from Fat 20); Total Fat 2.5g (Saturated Fat 0g); Cholesterol 0mg; Sodium 250mg; Total Carbohydrate 26g (Dietary Fiber 3g); Protein 2g

Easy Grilled Vegetables

Prep Time: 25 min   Start to Finish: 1 hr 25 min   6 Servings

12 pattypan squash, about 1 inch in diameter
2 medium red or green bell peppers, each cut into 6 pieces
1 large red onion, cut into ½-inch slices
⅓ cup reduced-fat Italian dressing
Freshly ground pepper, if desired

1 In 13×9-inch (3-quart) glass baking dish, place squash, bell peppers and onion. Pour dressing over vegetables. Cover and let stand 1 hour to blend flavors.

2 Heat coals or gas grill for direct heat. Remove vegetables from marinade; reserve marinade. Place vegetables in grill basket (grill "wok") or directly on grill rack.

3 Cover and grill vegetables over medium heat 10 to 15 minutes, shaking basket or turning vegetables and brushing with marinade 2 or 3 times, until crisp-tender. Sprinkle with pepper.

You can use one medium zucchini, cut into 1-inch pieces, in place of the pattypan squash. If you like mushrooms, go ahead and add them for the last 10 minutes of grilling.

1 Serving: Calories 80 (Calories from Fat 25); Total Fat 3g (Saturated Fat 0g); Cholesterol 0mg; Sodium 170mg; Total Carbohydrate 11g (Dietary Fiber 3g); Protein 2g

Grilled Corn with Chile-Lime Spread

Prep Time: 25 min   Start to Finish: 30 min   8 Servings

½ cup butter or margarine, softened
½ teaspoon grated lime peel
3 tablespoons lime juice
1 to 2 teaspoons ground red chiles or chili powder
8 ears fresh corn with husks

1 Heat coals or gas grill. In small bowl, mix all ingredients except corn.

2 Remove large outer husks from each ear of corn; gently pull back inner husks and remove silk. Spread each ear of corn with about 2 teaspoons butter mixture; reserve remaining butter mixture. Pull husks up over ears.

3 Place corn on grill. Cook uncovered over medium heat 10 to 15 minutes, turning frequently, until tender. Let stand 5 minutes. Serve corn with remaining butter mixture.

1 Serving: Calories 230 (Calories from Fat 120); Total Fat 13g (Saturated Fat 8g); Cholesterol 30mg; Sodium 105mg; Total Carbohydrate 26g (Dietary Fiber 4g); Protein 4g

Portabella Mushrooms with Herbs

Prep Time: 20 min   Start to Finish: 1 hr 30 min   4 Servings

2 tablespoons olive or vegetable oil
1 tablespoon balsamic vinegar
1 teaspoon chopped fresh or ¼ teaspoon dried oregano leaves
1 teaspoon chopped fresh or ¼ teaspoon dried thyme leaves
⅛ teaspoon salt
1 clove garlic, finely chopped
4 fresh portabella mushroom caps (about 4 inches in diameter)
¼ cup crumbled feta cheese with herbs

1 In large glass or plastic bowl or resealable plastic food-storage bag, mix oil, vinegar, oregano, thyme, salt and garlic. Add mushrooms; turn to coat. Cover dish or seal bag and refrigerate 1 hour.

2 Heat coals or gas grill for direct heat. Remove mushrooms from marinade (mushrooms will absorb most of the marinade). Cover and grill mushrooms over medium heat 8 to 10 minutes or until tender. Sprinkle with cheese.

This is a great side dish to serve with almost any grilled meat. Or serve it as a first course.

1 Serving: Calories 110 (Calories from Fat 80); Total Fat 9g (Saturated Fat 2.5g); Cholesterol 10mg; Sodium 180mg; Total Carbohydrate 4g (Dietary Fiber 0g); Protein 3g

Dilled Cucumber-Tomato Salad

Prep Time: 15 min   Start to Finish: 15 min   5 Servings (½ cup each)

¼ cup plain yogurt
1 small clove garlic, finely chopped
1½ teaspoon chopped fresh or ½ teaspoon dried dill weed
¼ teaspoon sugar
⅛ teaspoon salt
3 large plum (Roma) tomatoes, seeded, diced (1½ cups)
1 medium cucumber, peeled, seeded and cubed (1 cup)

1 In medium bowl, mix yogurt, garlic, dill weed, sugar and salt.

2 Fold in tomatoes and cucumber. Serve immediately.

1 Serving: Calories 25 (Calories from Fat 0); Total Fat 0g (Saturated Fat 0g); Cholesterol 0mg; Sodium 75mg; Total Carbohydrate 4g (Dietary Fiber 0g); Protein 1g

Lime-Mint Melon Salad

Prep Time: 20 min   Start to Finish: 2 hrs 20 min   6 Servings

1½ cups ½-inch cubes honeydew melon (½ medium)
1½ cups ½-inch cubes cantaloupe (½ medium)
1 teaspoon grated lime peel
3 tablespoons lime juice
2 tablespoons chopped fresh or 1 tablespoon dried mint leaves
1 teaspoon honey
¼ teaspoon salt

1 In medium glass or plastic bowl, toss all ingredients.

2 Cover and refrigerate about 2 hours or until chilled.

Select cantaloupe and honeydew melon by smelling the soft stem end. A sweet fruity fragrance means the melon is ripe. Store both varieties of melon at room temperature until ripe, then keep them in the refrigerator.

1 Serving: Calories 40 (Calories from Fat 0); Total Fat 0g (Saturated Fat 0g); Cholesterol 0mg; Sodium 110mg; Total Carbohydrate 9g (Dietary Fiber 0g); Protein 0g

Asian Slaw

Prep Time: 15 min   Start to Finish: 45 min   6 Servings (½ cup each)

4 cups thinly sliced Chinese (napa) cabbage
½ medium red bell pepper, thinly sliced
½ medium cucumber, seeded, thinly sliced
¼ cup citrus vinaigrette dressing
2 tablespoons low-sodium teriyaki sauce

1 In large bowl, mix cabbage, bell pepper and cucumber.

2 In small bowl, mix dressing and teriyaki sauce. Pour over cabbage mixture; toss to coat. Refrigerate at least 30 minutes before serving.

If low-sodium teriyaki sauce is not available, use low-sodium soy sauce.

1 Serving: Calories 40 (Calories from Fat 15); Total Fat 1.5g (Saturated Fat 0g); Cholesterol 0mg; Sodium 300mg; Total Carbohydrate 6g (Dietary Fiber 1g); Protein 1g

Tortellini, Broccoli and Bacon Salad

Prep Time: 25 min   Start to Finish: 1 hr 25 min   24 Servings (about ½ cup each)

2 bags (19 oz each) frozen cheese-filled tortellini
4 cups broccoli florets
2 cups cherry tomatoes, each cut in half
2 tablespoons chopped fresh chives
1 cup reduced-fat coleslaw dressing
1 lb bacon, crisply cooked, crumbled
¼ cup sunflower nuts

1 Cook and drain tortellini as directed on package. Rinse with cold water; drain.

2 In very large (4-quart) bowl, mix tortellini, broccoli, tomatoes, chives and dressing. Cover and refrigerate at least 1 hour to blend flavors.

3 Just before serving, stir in bacon. Sprinkle with nuts.

1 Serving: Calories 160 (Calories from Fat 80); Total Fat 9g (Saturated Fat 2.5g); Cholesterol 45mg; Sodium 340mg; Total Carbohydrate 14g (Dietary Fiber 1g); Protein 6g

Picnic Pasta Salad

Prep Time: 20 min   Start to Finish: 2 hrs 20 min   26 Servings (½ cup each)

1 package (16 oz) bow-tie (farfalle) pasta
1 can (8 oz) tomato sauce
1 cup Italian dressing
1 tablespoon chopped fresh or 1 teaspoon dried basil leaves
1 tablespoon chopped fresh or 1 teaspoon dried oregano leaves
1 cup sliced fresh mushrooms (3 oz)
5 plum (Roma) tomatoes, coarsely chopped (1½ cups)
1 large cucumber, coarsely chopped (1½ cups)
1 medium red onion, chopped (1½ cups)
1 can (2.25 oz) sliced ripe olives, drained

1 Cook and drain pasta as directed on package. Rinse with cold water; drain.

2 In large bowl, mix tomato sauce, dressing, basil and oregano. Add pasta and remaining ingredients; toss. Cover and refrigerate at least 2 hours until chilled but no longer than 48 hours.

1 Serving: Calories 120 (Calories from Fat 40); Total Fat 4.5g (Saturated Fat 0g); Cholesterol 0mg; Sodium 220mg; Total Carbohydrate 17g (Dietary Fiber 2g); Protein 3g

Don't like mushrooms? Go ahead and use roasted red bell pepper slices instead.

Mediterranean Potato Salad

Prep Time: 25 min   Start to Finish: 25 min   12 Servings (½ cup each)

1½ lb medium red potatoes, cut in half
3 slices bacon
¾ cup red or yellow grape tomatoes
¼ cup chopped onion
¼ cup sliced ripe olives
½ cup fat-free Italian dressing
1 tablespoon cider vinegar
1 tablespoon chopped fresh Italian parsley, if desired

1 In 3-quart saucepan, heat 1 inch water to boiling. Add potatoes. Cover and heat to boiling; reduce heat. Cover and simmer 10 to 15 minutes or until tender; drain. Cool slightly. Cut potatoes into ¾-inch cubes; place in large bowl.

2 Meanwhile, line microwavable plate with microwavable paper towel. Place bacon on paper towel; top with another microwavable paper towel. Microwave on High 2 to 3 minutes or until bacon is crisp. Crumble bacon.

3 Stir bacon, tomatoes, onion and olives into warm cubed potatoes. In small bowl, mix dressing and vinegar; pour over potato mixture, stirring gently to coat vegetables. Sprinkle with parsley. Serve warm or cool.

Serve this delicious side with grilled turkey or chicken sausage for an easy summer meal!

1 Serving: Calories 60 (Calories from Fat 15); Total Fat 1.5g (Saturated Fat 0g); Cholesterol 0mg; Sodium 170mg; Total Carbohydrate 12g (Dietary Fiber 2g); Protein 2g

Smoked Sausage Baked Beans

Prep Time: 10 min   Start to Finish: 1 hr 10 min   24 Servings

2 cans (5.5 oz each) baked beans
1 ring (1 lb) fully cooked smoked sausage, cubed
2 jalapeño chiles, seeded, finely chopped
1 tablespoon ground cumin
1 tablespoon chili powder

1 Heat oven to 350°F. In ungreased 4-quart casserole or nonstick Dutch oven, mix all ingredients.

2 Bake uncovered 45 to 60 minutes or until thoroughly heated and bubbly.

You can make these beans in advance, using a slow cooker, then bring it along to keep the beans warm. In 5- to 6-quart slow cooker, mix all ingredients. Cover and cook on Low heat setting 4 to 5 hours (or High heat setting 2 to 2½ hours) until thoroughly heated and desired consistency.

1 Serving: Calories 180 (Calories from Fat 60); Total Fat 7g (Saturated Fat 2.5g); Cholesterol 20mg; Sodium 750mg; Total Carbohydrate 26g (Dietary Fiber 7g); Protein 9g

California Citrus Broccoli Slaw

Prep Time: 20 min   Start to Finish: 20 min   12 Servings

Broccoli Slaw

1 bag (16 oz) broccoli slaw
1 small jicama, peeled, cut into julienne strips (2 cups)
3 oranges
1 small red onion, cut in half, thinly sliced (1 cup)
⅔ cup chopped fresh cilantro

Citrus Dressing

3 tablespoons vegetable oil
3 tablespoons lemon juice
4 teaspoons sugar
1½ teaspoons grated orange peel
⅛ teaspoon salt

1 In large bowl, mix broccoli slaw and jicama. Peel oranges with sharp paring knife; cut into ¼-inch slices. Cut each slice into fourths. Add oranges, onion and cilantro to broccoli mixture.

2 In a tightly covered container, prepare dressing by shaking all of the ingredients; pour over salad and toss. Serve immediately, or cover and refrigerate up to 24 hours.

Jicama is a crunchy root vegetable with a sweet, nutty flavor that's popular in Mexican cuisine. It keeps its pretty ivory color, which makes it a natural choice to use in salads like this one.

1 Serving: Calories 80 (Calories from Fat 30); Total Fat 3.5g (Saturated Fat 0g); Cholesterol 0mg; Sodium 35mg; Total Carbohydrate 10g (Dietary Fiber 4g); Protein 2g

Lemon Tea Slush

Cranberry-Mint Iced Tea

Pineapple Limeade

Not-So-"Hard" Lemonade

Raspberry Lemonade

Citrus Spritzers

Italian Fruit Punch

Colada Cooler Punch

Iced Hazlenut Coffee Coolers

Peachy Mimosas

Dreamy Tropical Cream Fizz

Cosmo Slush

Strawberry-Rhubarb Slush

Layered Strawberry Shakes

Key Lime–Banana Smoothies

Creamy Mango Smoothies

Frosty Guava-Peach Sippers

Mangoritas

Frozen Strawberry Margaritas

Raspberry-Apricot Sangria

5
refreshing drinks

Lemon Tea Slush

Prep Time: 20 min ▪ Start to Finish: 24 hrs 40 min ▪ 12 Servings (1 cup each)

5 cups water
2 tea bags green tea
1 cup sugar
1 can (12 oz) frozen lemonade concentrate, thawed
1 cup vodka
1 bottle (1 liter) sparkling water, chilled
Lemon slices, if desired

1 In 2-cup microwavable measuring cup, microwave 1 cup of the water on High until boiling. Add tea bags to boiling water; let steep 10 minutes. Remove tea bags; cool tea.

2 Meanwhile, in 2-quart saucepan, heat remaining 4 cups water to boiling. Stir in sugar until dissolved. Remove from heat; cool 20 minutes.

3 In 3-quart plastic container, mix tea, sugar water, lemonade concentrate and vodka. Cover and freeze at least 24 hours.

4 To serve, place ⅔ cup slush in each glass and fill with ⅓ cup sparkling water; stir. Garnish with lemon slices.

Store the slush in a covered container in the freezer for up to 1 month.

1 Serving: Calories 120 (Calories from Fat 0); Total Fat 0g (Saturated Fat 0g); Cholesterol 0mg; Sodium 0mg; Total Carbohydrate 30g (Dietary Fiber 0g); Protein 0g

Cranberry-Mint Iced Tea

Prep Time: 15 min ▪ Start to Finish: 15 min ▪ 6 Servings (1 cup each)

6 cups cranberry juice cocktail (not unsweetened cranberry juice)
4 tea bags black tea
10 mint leaves (1 inch each)
2 tablespoons sugar

1 Heat cranberry juice cocktail to boiling in 2-quart saucepan. Pour over tea bags and mint in 2-quart glass measuring cup or heatproof pitcher. Let steep 5 to 10 minutes.

2 Strain tea mixture. Stir in sugar. Serve tea over ice. Add more sugar if desired.

To keep tea from becoming cloudy, heat the liquid and steep the tea in nonreactive utensils, such as glass or stainless steel.

1 Serving: Calories 160 (Calories from Fat 0); Total Fat 0g (Saturated Fat 0g); Cholesterol 0mg; Sodium 5mg; Total Carbohydrate 41g (Dietary Fiber 0g); Protein 0g

Pineapple Limeade

Prep Time: 10 min ▪ Start to Finish: 10 min ▪ 16 Servings (about 1 cup each)

1 cup sugar
6 cups pineapple juice, chilled
1 cup lime juice
2 liters sparkling water, chilled
Lime slices, if desired

1 In large glass or plastic pitcher, mix sugar and juices. Pour half of mixture into another large pitcher.

2 Just before serving, stir 1 liter sparkling water into each pitcher. Serve over ice. Garnish with lime slices.

1 Serving: Calories 110 (Calories from Fat 0); Total Fat 0g (Saturated Fat 0g); Cholesterol 0mg; Sodium 0mg; Total Carbohydrate 26g (Dietary Fiber 0g); Protein 0g

Not-So-"Hard" Lemonade

Prep Time: 15 min ▪ Start to Finish: 2 hrs 15 min ▪ 6 Servings (2/3 cup each)

3 orange slices, each cut in half
3 lemon slices, each cut in half
3 small strawberries, cut lengthwise in half
6 green grapes
5 bottles (11.2 oz each) lemon malt beverage, chilled
1/3 cup grenadine syrup

1 Remove any seeds from orange and lemon slices.

2 In ungreased 15×10×1-inch pan, place orange slices, lemon slices, strawberry halves and grapes in single layer. Freeze at least 2 hours until fruit is frozen.

3 When ready to serve, pour malt beverage into each of 6 tall glasses. Drizzle 1 tablespoon grenadine syrup into each glass. Place orange slice, lemon slice, strawberry half and 1 grape into each glass.

Frozen chunks of fresh fruit make colorful and tasty "ice cubes" for any summertime beverage.

1 Serving: Calories 120 (Calories from Fat 0); Total Fat 0g (Saturated Fat 0g); Cholesterol 0mg; Sodium 35mg; Total Carbohydrate 29g (Dietary Fiber 2g); Protein 1g

Raspberry Lemonade

Prep Time: 20 min ▪ Start to Finish: 2 hrs 20 min ▪ 6 Servings (about 1 cup each)

Raspberry Lemonade
¾ cup sugar
4 cups water
1 cup fresh lemon juice (about 4 lemons)
1 box (10 oz) frozen raspberries in syrup, thawed

Raspberry Ice Cubes
Reserved raspberries
¾ cup water

1 In 1-quart saucepan, mix sugar and ½ cup of the water. Cook over medium heat, stirring once, until sugar is dissolved. Cool to room temperature.

2 In 2-quart nonmetal pitcher, mix cooled sugar syrup, lemon juice and the remaining 3½ cups water. Place raspberries in strainer over small bowl to drain (do not press berries through strainer). Reserve berries for raspberry ice cubes. Stir raspberry liquid into lemon mixture; refrigerate.

3 Make raspberry ice cubes by spooning raspberries evenly into 12 sections of ice-cube tray. Divide water evenly among sections with raspberries. Freeze about 2 hours or until firm.

4 Serve lemonade over ice cubes.

1 Serving: Calories 160 (Calories from Fat 0); Total Fat 0g (Saturated Fat 0g); Cholesterol 0mg; Sodium 10mg; Total Carbohydrate 40g (Dietary Fiber 2g); Protein 0g

Citrus Spritzers

Prep Time: 10 min ▪ Start to Finish: 10 min ▪ 8 Servings (about ¾ cup each)

2 cups cold water
1 can (6 oz) frozen orange juice concentrate, thawed
¾ cup frozen (thawed) grapefruit juice concentrate (from 12-oz can)
1 bottle (1 liter) sparkling water, chilled
Orange slices, if desired
Fresh mint leaves, if desired

1 In large pitcher, mix cold water, orange juice concentrate, grapefruit juice concentrate and sparkling water.

2 Serve spritzers over ice. Garnish each serving with orange slice and mint leaf.

Make garnish "kabobs" by threading thin slices of lime, lemon or orange on decorative toothpicks.

1 Serving: Calories 70 (Calories from Fat 0); Total Fat 0g (Saturated Fat 0g); Cholesterol 0mg; Sodium 0mg; Total Carbohydrate 17g (Dietary Fiber 0g); Protein 1g

Italian Fruit Punch

Prep Time: 15 min ▪ Start to Finish: 10 hrs ▪ 28 Servings (½ cup each)

Ice Ring

1 can (12 oz) frozen lemonade concentrate, thawed
4 cans water
2 cups (about 12 large) frozen strawberries
2 lemons, cut into ¼-inch slices, slices cut in half

Punch

1 can (12 oz) frozen lemonade concentrate, thawed
1 can (12 oz) frozen limeade concentrate, thawed
3 cups cold water
4 cups lemon-lime carbonated beverage, chilled
1 bottle (1 liter) club soda, chilled

1 In pitcher, mix 1 can lemonade concentrate and 4 cans water. Pour 2 cups of the lemonade into 12-cup fluted tube cake pan. Freeze in coldest section of freezer about 45 minutes or until thin coating of ice forms on surface. Crack ice crust with small, sharp knife to expose liquid underneath. Working quickly, place strawberries and lemon slices in liquid, making sure each piece is partially submerged. Return pan to freezer about 1 hour or until lemonade is frozen solid. Remove from freezer and add remaining lemonade. Freeze at least 8 hours or overnight.

2 In 2-quart pitcher, mix 1 can lemonade concentrate, the limeade concentrate and 3 cups water. Refrigerate until ready to use.

3 Just before serving, pour limeade mixture, lemon-lime beverage and club soda into punch bowl. Dip pan with ice ring very quickly into warm water, then turn upside down to release ice ring. Float ring in punch bowl.

1 Serving: Calories 90 (Calories from Fat 0); Total Fat 0g (Saturated Fat 0g); Cholesterol 0mg; Sodium 15mg; Total Carbohydrate 23g (Dietary Fiber 0g); Protein 0g

Colada Cooler Punch

Prep Time: 10 min ▪ Start to Finish: 10 min ▪ 24 Servings (1 cup each)

2 cans (12 oz each) frozen piña colada concentrate, thawed
2 cans (12 oz each) frozen white grape juice concentrate, thawed
6 cups cold water
12 cups (about 3 liters) lemon-lime carbonated beverage
Lemon and lime slices

1 In large glass or plastic container, mix piña colada and juice concentrates. Stir in water.

2 Just before serving, pour into punch bowl. Add lemon-lime beverage and lemon and lime slices. Serve over ice.

Make grape ice cubes by putting 1 or 2 grapes in each section of an ice-cube tray. Cover with water and freeze.

1 Serving: Calories 120 (Calories from Fat 0); Total Fat 0g (Saturated Fat 0g); Cholesterol 0mg; Sodium 15mg; Total Carbohydrate 30g (Dietary Fiber 0g); Protein 0g

Iced Hazelnut Coffee Coolers

Prep Time: 10 min ▪ Start to Finish: 3 hrs 10 min ▪ 12 Servings (1½ cups each)

⅔ cup instant coffee granules or crystals
¾ cup hazelnut-flavored liquid nondairy creamer
1 cup sugar
1 cup water
¼ teaspoon ground cinnamon
8 cups milk
48 water ice cubes

1 In medium bowl, stir coffee, creamer, sugar, water and cinnamon until coffee is dissolved.

2 Pour coffee mixture into 2 ice-cube trays. Freeze at least 3 hours until hardened. Transfer frozen coffee cubes to plastic storage container or freezer bag.

3 For each serving, place 2 coffee cubes, ⅔ cup milk and 4 water ice cubes in blender. Cover and blend on high speed about 20 seconds or until blended and slightly slushy. Pour into glass.

For an extra special touch, top this coffee cooler with a dollop of whipped cream, a dash of ground cinnamon and some hazelnuts (filberts).

1 Serving: Calories 170 (Calories from Fat 40); Total Fat 4.5g (Saturated Fat 2g); Cholesterol 15mg; Sodium 80mg; Total Carbohydrate 28g (Dietary Fiber 0g); Protein 6g

Peachy Mimosas

Prep Time: 5 min ▮ Start to Finish: 5 min ▮ 12 Servings (⅔ cup each)

2 cups orange juice, chilled
2 cups peach nectar, chilled
1 bottle (750 ml) regular or nonalcoholic dry champagne or sparkling wine, chilled

1 In 1½-quart pitcher, mix orange juice and peach nectar.

2 Pour champagne into glasses until half full. Fill glasses with juice mixture.

1 Serving: Calories 100 (Calories from Fat 0); Total Fat 0g (Saturated Fat 0g); Cholesterol 0mg; Sodium 10mg; Total Carbohydrate 11g (Dietary Fiber 0g); Protein 0g

Dreamy Tropical Cream Fizz

Prep Time: 10 min ▪ Start to Finish: 1 hr 10 min ▪ 6 Servings (1 cup each)

¼ cup shredded coconut
2 cups tropical juice blend
½ cup sugar
¼ cup lime juice
12 to 14 ice cubes
1 ½ cups club soda
1 pint coconut ice cream, coconut sorbet or vanilla ice cream

1 Place coconut in food processor or blender. Cover and process until coconut is in small pieces. Place coconut in shallow dish. Dip rims of six 12-ounce stemmed glasses into water, then dip into coconut to coat. Chill glasses in freezer at least 1 hour before serving.

2 Place tropical juice blend, sugar, lime juice and ice cubes in blender. Cover and blend on high speed about 45 seconds or until smooth. Pour mixture into glasses.

3 Pour ¼ cup club soda into juice mixture in each glass. Add 1 large scoop ice cream to each glass. Garnish with remaining coconut if desired.

1 Serving: Calories 230 (Calories from Fat 60); Total Fat 7g (Saturated Fat 4.5g); Cholesterol 20mg; Sodium 50mg; Total Carbohydrate 41g (Dietary Fiber 0g); Protein 2g

Cosmo Slush

Prep Time: 10 min ▪ Start to Finish: 8 hrs 10 min ▪ 14 Servings (½ cup each)

6 oz frozen (thawed) limeade concentrate (from 12-oz can)
3 tablespoons powdered sugar
2 cups citrus-flavored vodka or orange juice
1 cup orange-flavored liqueur or orange juice
4 cups 100% cranberry juice blend

1 In blender, place limeade concentrate and powdered sugar. Cover and blend on high speed until well mixed. Add vodka and orange liqueur. Cover and blend until well mixed.

2 In 13×9-inch glass baking dish, stir limeade mixture and cranberry juice until well mixed.

3 Cover and freeze at least 8 hours until slushy. Stir before serving.

For vibrant flavor and color, make this slush with 100% cranberry juice, not cranberry juice cocktail.

1 Serving: Calories 90 (Calories from Fat 0); Total Fat 0g (Saturated Fat 0g); Cholesterol 0mg; Sodium 0mg; Total Carbohydrate 23g (Dietary Fiber 0g); Protein 0g

Strawberry-Rhubarb Slush

Prep Time: 20 min ▪ Start to Finish: 8 hrs 20 min ▪ 16 Servings (1 cup each)

1 bag (16 oz) frozen rhubarb or 3 cups chopped fresh rhubarb
1 cup sugar
2 packages (10 oz each) frozen sweetened strawberries, slightly thawed
1½ cups vodka
1 can (12 oz) lemon-lime carbonated beverage
1 bottle (2 liters) lemon-lime carbonated beverage, chilled
Fresh strawberries, if desired

1 In 3-quart saucepan, heat rhubarb and sugar to boiling over medium heat, stirring occasionally. Cook 8 to 10 minutes, stirring occasionally, until rhubarb is very tender. Stir in strawberries.

2 Spoon into blender half of the strawberry mixture. Cover and blend on high speed until smooth. Pour into large nonmetal container. Cover and blend remaining strawberry mixture; add to container. Stir in vodka and 12-ounce can of lemon-lime beverage. Freeze at least 8 hours until frozen and slushy.

3 For each serving, stir together ½ cup frozen mixture and ½ cup chilled lemon-lime beverage in tall glass until slushy. Garnish with strawberry.

Turn this recipe into a slushy punch for your next party. Spoon the slush mixture into a large punch bowl, then stir in the carbonated beverage. This is a handy and refreshing beverage when serving a large number of guests.

1 Serving: Calories 170 (Calories from Fat 0); Total Fat 0g (Saturated Fat 0g); Cholesterol 0mg; Sodium 20mg; Total Carbohydrate 41g (Dietary Fiber 1g); Protein 0g

Layered Strawberry Shakes

Prep Time: 20 min ▪ Start to Finish: 20 min ▪ 6 Servings (about ¾ cup each)

1 container (16 oz) fresh strawberries, coarsely chopped
4 cups vanilla ice cream
¾ cup milk

1 In blender, place strawberries. Cover and blend on high speed about 1 minute, stopping blender occasionally to stir, until smooth. Remove from blender. Rinse blender.

2 In blender, place ice cream and milk. Cover and blend on high speed about 2 minutes, stopping blender occasionally to stir, until smooth and creamy.

3 When ready to serve, in each of six 10- to 12-ounce glasses, layer ¼ cup blended ice cream, ⅓ cup strawberry puree and another ¼ cup blended ice cream.

Make these shakes the centerpiece of a kids' party along with peanut butter and jelly sandwiches, grape clusters and sugar wafer cookies.

1 Serving: Calories 230 (Calories from Fat 100); Total Fat 11g (Saturated Fat 7g); Cholesterol 45mg; Sodium 90mg; Total Carbohydrate 29g (Dietary Fiber 2g); Protein 5g

Key Lime–Banana Smoothies

Prep Time: 10 min ▮ Start to Finish: 10 min ▮ 2 Servings (1 cup each)

1 container (6 oz) Key lime pie low-fat yogurt
1 ripe banana, sliced
½ cup milk
1 tablespoon lime juice
¼ teaspoon dry lemon-lime-flavored soft drink mix (from 0.13-oz package)
1 cup vanilla frozen yogurt

1 In blender, place all ingredients except frozen yogurt. Cover and blend on high speed until smooth.

2 Add frozen yogurt. Cover and blend until smooth.

For the best banana flavor, choose bananas that have flecks of brown on the skin. Bananas that are too green will not be as sweet or flavorful.

1 Serving: Calories 340 (Calories from Fat 40); Total Fat 4.5g (Saturated Fat 2.5g); Cholesterol 15mg; Sodium 160mg; Total Carbohydrate 64g (Dietary Fiber 2g); Protein 12g

Creamy Mango Smoothies

Prep Time: 10 min ▪ Start to Finish: 10 min ▪ 6 Servings (1 cup each)

2 mangoes, peeled, chopped (2 cups)
2 cups mango sorbet
2 containers (6 oz each) French vanilla yogurt
1½ cups milk

1 In blender, place all ingredients. Cover and blend on high speed until smooth.

For the best flavor, choose ripe mangoes. The skins should be yellow with blushes of red.

1 Serving: Calories 220 (Calories from Fat 20); Total Fat 2g (Saturated Fat 1g); Cholesterol 5mg; Sodium 75mg; Total Carbohydrate 46g (Dietary Fiber 2g); Protein 5g

Frosty Guava-Peach Sippers

Prep Time: 10 min ▪ Start to Finish: 10 min ▪ 4 Servings (1 cup each)

1 can (10 oz) frozen fuzzy navel drink mix
1 cup guava juice or guava blend juice
¼ cup dark rum or guava juice
2 cups cracked ice

1 In blender, place all ingredients except ice. Cover and blend on high speed until well mixed.

2 Add ice. Cover and blend until smooth and slushy.

Fuzzy navel drinks combine the summer-fresh flavors of peach and orange. You can find the drink mix near the other frozen juices and beverages at the supermarket.

1 Serving: Calories 40 (Calories from Fat 0); Total Fat 0g (Saturated Fat 0g); Cholesterol 0mg; Sodium 0mg; Total Carbohydrate 10g (Dietary Fiber 0g); Protein 0g

Mangoritas

Prep Time: 10 min ▪ Start to Finish: 10 min ▪ 4 Servings (1 cup each)

1 can (10 oz) frozen margarita drink mix
1 cup mango nectar
½ cup tequila or mango nectar
2 cups cracked ice

1 In blender, place all ingredients except ice. Cover and blend on high speed until well mixed.

2 Add ice. Cover and blend until smooth and slushy.

The rims of margarita glasses are typically coated with lime juice and dipped in coarse salt. For these sweeter "mangoritas," coat the rims with lime juice and dip in coarse sugar.

1 Serving: Calories 210 (Calories from Fat 0); Total Fat 0g (Saturated Fat 0g); Cholesterol 0mg; Sodium 0mg; Total Carbohydrate 53g (Dietary Fiber 0g); Protein 0g

Frozen Strawberry Margaritas

Prep Time: 10 min ▪ Start to Finish: 24 hrs 10 min ▪ 10 Servings

½ can (12 oz) frozen limeade concentrate, thawed
1 box (10 oz) frozen strawberries in syrup, thawed, undrained
3 cups water
¾ cup tequila or orange juice
1 bottle (1 liter) lemon-lime carbonated beverage, chilled

1 In blender, place limeade concentrate and strawberries. Cover; blend until smooth. Stir in water and tequila. Pour into 2-quart plastic container. Cover; freeze 24 hours or until slushy.

2 If orange juice was used, let stand at room temperature 2 hours before serving. To serve, place ⅔ cup slush in each glass and fill with ⅓ cup lemon-lime beverage; stir.

1 Serving: Calories 140 (Calories from Fat 0); Total Fat 0g (Saturated Fat 0g); Cholesterol 0mg; Sodium 15mg; Total Carbohydrate 26g (Dietary Fiber 0g); Protein 0g

Raspberry-Apricot Sangria

Prep Time: 15 min ▪ Start to Finish: 15 min ▪ 9 Servings (1 cup each)

1 package (10 oz) frozen sweetened raspberries, thawed
2 cups apricot nectar
1 bottle (750 ml) white wine or nonalcoholic white wine, chilled
¼ cup apricot brandy, if desired
2 cans (12 oz each) lemon-lime carbonated beverage, chilled
½ pint (1 cup) fresh raspberries
Lemon and/or orange slices, if desired

1 In blender, place thawed raspberries. Cover and blend on high speed until pureed. Press blended raspberries through a strainer into small bowl, using wooden spoon; discard seeds.

2 In 2-quart nonmetal pitcher or container, mix raspberry puree, nectar, wine and brandy. Just before serving, add lemon-lime beverage, fresh raspberries and lemon slices. Serve over ice.

Sangria comes from Spain and was originally made with red wine and fruit juices. White or blush wines offer a lighter version of this summer drink.

1 Serving: Calories 165 (Calories from Fat 0); Total Fat 0g (Saturated Fat 0g); Cholesterol 0mg; Sodium 20mg; Total Carbohydrate 29g (Dietary Fiber 3g); Protein 1g

Helpful Nutrition and Cooking Information

Recommended intake for a daily diet of 2,000 calories as set by the Food and Drug Administration

Total Fat	Less than 65g
Saturated Fat	Less than 20g
Cholesterol	Less than 300mg
Sodium	Less than 2,400mg
Total Carbohydrate	300g
Dietary Fiber	25g

Calculating Nutrition Information

- The first ingredient is used wherever a choice is given (such as $1/3$ cup sour cream or plain yogurt).

- The first ingredient amount is used wherever a range is given (such as 2 to 3 teaspoons).

- The first serving number was used wherever a range is given (such as 4 to 6 servings).

- "If desired" ingredients and recipe variations were not included (such as sprinkle with brown sugar, if desired).

- Only the amount of a marinade or frying oil that is absorbed by the food during preparation was calculated.

Ingredients Used in Recipe Testing and Nutrition Calculations

The following ingredients, based on most commonly purchased ingredients, are used unless indicated otherwise:

- Large eggs, 2% milk, 80%-lean ground beef, canned chicken broth and vegetable oil spread containing at least 65% fat when margarine is used.

- Solid vegetable shortening (not butter, margarine, or nonstick cooking spray) is used to grease pans.

Equipment Used in Recipe Testing

- Cookware and bakeware without nonstick coatings were used, unless otherwise indicated.

- No dark-colored, black or insulated bakeware was used.

- When a pan is specified, a metal pan was used; a baking dish or pie plate means ovenproof glass was used.

- An electric hand mixer was used for mixing when mixer speeds are specified.

Metric Conversion Guide

VOLUME

U.S. Units	Canadian Metric	Australian Metric
¹/₄ teaspoon	1 mL	1 ml
¹/₂ teaspoon	2 mL	2 ml
1 teaspoon	5 mL	5 ml
1 tablespoon	15 mL	20 ml
¹/₄ cup	50 mL	60 ml
¹/₃ cup	75 mL	80 ml
¹/₂ cup	125 mL	125 ml
²/₃ cup	150 mL	170 ml
³/₄ cup	175 mL	190 ml
1 cup	250 mL	250 ml
1 quart	1 liter	1 liter
1 ¹/₂ quarts	1.5 liters	1.5 liters
2 quarts	2 liters	2 liters
2 ¹/₂ quarts	2.5 liters	2.5 liters
3 quarts	3 liters	3 liters
4 quarts	4 liters	4 liters

WEIGHT

U.S. Units	Canadian Metric	Australian Metric
1 ounce	30 grams	30 grams
2 ounces	55 grams	60 grams
3 ounces	85 grams	90 grams
4 ounces (¹/₄ pound)	115 grams	125 grams
8 ounces (¹/₂ pound)	225 grams	225 grams
16 ounces (1 pound)	455 grams	500 grams
1 pound	455 grams	¹/₂ kilogram

MEASUREMENTS

Inches	Centimeters
1	2.5
2	5.0
3	7.5
4	10.0
5	12.5
6	15.0
7	17.5
8	20.5
9	23.0
10	25.5
11	28.0
12	30.5
13	33.0

TEMPERATURES

Fahrenheit	Celsius
32°	0°
212°	100°
250°	120°
275°	140°
300°	150°
325°	160°
350°	180°
375°	190°
400°	200°
425°	220°
450°	230°
475°	240°
500°	260°

NOTE: The recipes in this cookbook have not been developed or tested using metric measures. When converting recipes to metric, some variations in quality may be noted.

Index

Page numbers in italics indicate illustrations.

Whatever's on the menu, make it easy with *Betty Crocker*

Betty Crocker
chicken tonight
100 Recipes for the Way You Really Cook

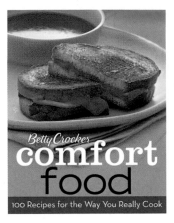

Betty Crocker
comfort food
100 Recipes for the Way You Really Cook

Betty Crocker
simply dessert
100 Recipes for the Way You Really Cook

Betty Crocker
food

Betty Crocker
party food
100 Recipes for the Way You Really Cook

Betty Crocker
quick fixes
100 Recipes for the Way You Really Cook